TAX-EFFICIENT WHITE COAT

THE S.W.A.N.™ APPROACH: HOW DOCTORS & DENTISTS CAN STOP THE TAX BLEED AND BUILD REAL WEALTH

FROM THE AUTHOR OF AMAZON'S #1 BESTSELLING BOOK, "EFFORTLESS WEALTH"

PAAVAN KOTINI

Foreword by
TRACY GAPIN

Foreword by
MICHELLE LAFRINERE

KOTINI MEDIA GROUP

.

PRAISE FOR THE BOOK

"*Tax Efficient White Coat*" by Paavan Kotini, empowers physicians and dentists to take control of their financial future with the same precision they bring to patient care. It's a powerful reminder that financial clarity isn't a luxury, it's essential for personal and professional well-being.In medicine, we're trained to diagnose and plan for our patients, yet rarely taught to do the same for our finances. Tax Efficient White Coat bridges that gap, offering a clear, strategic approach that every clinician can apply to build stability and freedom. Financial stress is one of the silent drivers of burnout in our profession. Tax Efficient White Coat provides a much-needed guide to reducing that burden and creating a sustainable, secure future for every medical professional."

- **Saraswathi Lakkasani**, MD, DEM, MEM, Gastroenterology, RWJBH Medical Group

"I found *Tax Efficient White Coat* incredibly insightful. Paavan's strategies helped me save and mitigate taxes significantly, giving me real financial clarity and peace of mind. I highly recommend this book to every doctor and dentist who wants to take control of their financial future. It's practical, smart, and empowering."

- **George Varkey**, DMD, CEO, United Smiles Dentistry

"As physicians, we dedicate years mastering medicine, yet receive little guidance on how to protect and grow the fruits of that work. *Tax Efficient White Coat* shines a light on the financial side of our profession-empowering doctors and medical professionals to make informed, strategic decisions that preserve wealth and create long-term stability. This is a must-read for anyone in healthcare seeking financial clarity and control."

- **Fernando Woll**, MD, Pulmonary and Sleep Center of the Valley

"First of all thank you for all your support with our tax strategy planning. Traditionally we have been paying tax without any good strategy being applied until the last couple of years where we learnt a lot from you. By applying these strategies we have saved a lot on our taxes. The best part is my CPA is also learning from this and encouraging his other clients to follow your strategies to help save more in taxes legally. Like you mentioned as an individual/ CPA we only know 2 % of tax savings plan and for the rest we need a strategist like you to help save taxes. Regarding this book [*Tax Efficient White Coat*] it's definitely an eye opener for me who has zero knowledge on tax strategy being in the medical field. It's in simple words especially for a person like me to understand. Best wishes for all your future endeavors and keep helping folks like me to help save on taxes and strategize accordingly."

- **Ramky Kavaserry**, PT, DPT, RVA Physical Therapy & Sports Rehab LLC

"I have been reading your book [*Tax Efficient White Coat*] whenever I had some time in between the patients at work. It is very well written and easy to understand to a financial illiterate like me. I truly wish I had some kind of financial planning course in my dental school. Reading this book is an eye opening experience for me about financial planning."

- **Srikanth Papisetti**, DMD, United Smiles Dentistry

"Wow, what a fantastic all-in-one resource from Paavan. *Tax-Efficient White Coat* is something that I would surely pass on to my children who are aspiring to be a doctor and a dentist. Financial literacy is something we do not learn in medical or dental schools but it is crucial for us to be successful financially. This book touches every aspect of wealth building strategies: saving, generating and protecting. The best part about the book is its laid-out strategy which provides a clear road map for financial success. I consider my time well spent reading it."

- **Vamsee Amirneni**, MD, Internist at OhioHealth Physician Group

"*Tax-Efficient White Coat* breaks down what every high-earning doctor should know but most were never taught —how to actually keep more of what we earn. It's not just tax tricks; it's mindset, structure, and strategy. As a dentist and business owner, I can tell you —understanding this side of finance is just as important as clinical skill if you want long-term freedom. This book is a reminder that smart wealth isn't about how much you make —it's about how efficiently you keep and grow it."

- **Naveen Chennupati**, DDS, Best Smiles Family Dentistry & Implant Center

"Practicing medicine, I never thought I was in the tax bracket to optimize my money like the ultra-wealthy. I restrained myself to maximizing retirement accounts, traditional investing, and begrudgingly hearing about last earnings call in the doctor's lounge. Paavan then opened a new door to me: tax efficiency. I'm sure his wisdom and strategies will provide you with the same excitement they have brought me in building a better financial life and legacy."

- **Vishal Mehta**, MD, Carolinas Hospitalist Group

"This book [*Tax Efficient White Coat*] was an excellent read—concise yet richly illustrative. It offers clear, practical examples that distinguish a deliberate, well-structured tax mitigation strategy from the reactive habit of merely extinguishing financial fires. The message is unmistakable: a proactive, planned approach consistently delivers stronger long-term outcomes."

- **Krishna and Sraavya Akella**, MD's, Springfield Clinic & Siu Women's Health Clinic

"Being an early career physician, financial planning is an extremely stressful aspect of life in which one receives very little guidance during training. Paavan and *Tax Efficient White Coat* provided much-needed guidance in the confusing world of finance and including all aspects including financial planning, tax-saving strategies, and wealth preservation. This is a must-read for any early-career and likely many mid-career health professional."

- **Vivak Master**, MD, Virginia Cardiovascular Specialists

"*Tax-Efficient White Coat* is an essential guide for every high-earning professional who wants to build lasting wealth without losing it all to taxes. With clarity, practicality, and empathy, Paavan Kotini demystifies complex tax concepts and turns them into actionable strategies. This book should be required reading for every physician and professional serious about financial independence."

- **Dr. Rajesh Devisetti**, DDS, Best Smiles Dentist

"Paavan's book [*Tax-Efficient White Coat*] finally brings clarity to a topic most of us in medicine shy away from—money and taxes. He breaks down complicated concepts through relatable stories and actionable advice. It's not just financial guidance; it's a guide to peace of mind."

- **Dr. Mansi Mehta**, DMD, FICOI, Affordable Dentures & Implants

To Madhuri, Nitya, and Prem —your love has illuminated my life and given it deeper meaning. You are the reason I strive to reach my fullest potential.

CONTENTS

Part I
THE DIAGNOSIS

CHAPTER 1

CHAPTER 2

Part II
THE ART OF TAX PLANNING

CHAPTER 3

CHAPTER 4

CHAPTER 5

CHAPTER 6

DISCLAIMER

The information contained in this book reflects the opinions and ideas of the author and is presented for general educational and informational purposes only. Although every effort has been made to ensure the accuracy and timeliness of the material, laws and regulations change frequently, and each individual's financial situation is unique. Consequently, neither the author nor the publisher can be held responsible for any errors, omissions, or outcomes arising from the use or misuse of the information provided.

Nothing in this book should be construed as personalized financial, tax, legal, investment, or professional advice. Readers should not act or refrain from acting based solely on the information contained herein without first consulting qualified professionals who can consider their specific circumstances and objectives. Any examples, figures, or references to past performance are illustrative only and do not guarantee future results.

All individuals and families described in this book are hypothetical composites based on the author's experience with countless families. These illustrative scenarios are designed solely to convey general principles; they do not depict specific persons, and any resemblance to real individuals is coincidental.

By reading and using this book, you acknowledge that you bear sole responsibility for your own financial decisions and that you agree to hold the author and publisher harmless against any and all claims or liabilities arising directly or indirectly from its contents.

FOREWORD BY TRACY GAPIN, MD

As physicians, we're trained to master the human body: to diagnose, to heal, to save lives. But despite all of our years of education, we're never taught how to take care of our own financial health.

We learn how to save others. No one ever teaches us how to save ourselves.

Most doctors I meet are brilliant, driven, compassionate and exhausted. We've sacrificed time, family, and freedom for a system that rewards us for working harder but never for thinking differently. We spend our lives serving patients while quietly bleeding financially, losing 35–45% of everything we earn to taxes every year.

It's a silent epidemic and it's killing more dreams than burnout ever could.

That's why Tax-Efficient White Coat is such an important book.

Paavan Kotini has built a roadmap that finally gives physicians the clarity and control we were never taught to have. He understands our world — the long hours, the endless charts, the hidden costs of "success." And he's created a system that empowers us to stop the financial bleeding and reclaim our freedom.

What makes this book different is its precision. It's not theory. It's not abstract financial jargon. It's a data-driven, physician-specific guide to taking control of your wealth with the same intentionality you bring to your patients' care. It's practical, actionable, and deeply human.

As someone who's spent the last two and a half decades helping high-performing professionals optimize their health and performance, , I've learned that the same principles that drive physical optimization also apply to financial freedom. Sustainable success doesn't come from quick fixes or hustle; it comes from building systems that create clarity, consistency, and confidence.

That's what Paavan's S.W.A.N.™ approach (Sleep Well At Night) delivers. It's about designing your financial life with the same precision and purpose you use to diagnose and treat your patients. It's about reclaiming your time, energy, and peace of mind so you can focus on what truly matters: your purpose, your impact, and your legacy.

Every physician deserves that.

The lessons in this book go far beyond taxes. They're about taking back ownership of your money, your time, and your future. They're about building legacy and freedom with the same purpose and precision that made you successful in the first place.

So as you read this book, don't just skim the numbers. Absorb the mindset. Let it challenge what you thought you knew about success. Because when you master this side of your life, you don't just gain financial control: you unlock the freedom to practice, live, and lead on your own terms.

This book isn't about escaping medicine. It's about empowering doctors to thrive within it. And that, to me, is a mission worth standing behind.

— **Tracy Gapin, MD, FACS**

Founder / CEO of the Gapin Institute for High Performance Health
Best-Selling Author of Male 2.0 and Codes of Longevity
Member of the American Academy of Anti-Aging, Age Management Medical Group, and International Peptide Society

GAINSWave Certified Success Provider
Creator of the proprietary Peak Launch Program

FOREWORD FROM MICHELLE LAFRINERE, CPA

For many physicians and dentists, taxes are treated like a routine obligation—something to address once a year, quickly sign, and hope for the best. But just as every dental or medical professional knows, reactive care is rarely the path to the best outcome.

A dentist would never advise a patient to "only come in when something hurts." Waiting until there is a problem leads to unnecessary pain, higher costs, and often limited options. The same is true with your taxes. If you only talk to your CPA at tax time, the planning window has closed and the opportunity to make meaningful changes is gone.

True tax planning—like preventative care—is proactive. It requires ongoing check-ins, strategy, and a focus on long-term health. I often tell clients: you should meet with your tax advisor at least twice a year, just like your six-month cleanings. Those intentional touchpoints create space to adjust, optimize, and plan ahead rather than diagnose problems after it's too late. Just like in dentistry, proactive care prevents small "cavities" from turning into painful and expensive root canals—tax planning works the same way.

Unfortunately, not all CPAs practice this way. Many simply file tax returns—reporting history rather than shaping your future. And for high-earning medical and dental professionals, the cost of reactive "tax filing" over strategic "tax planning" can be staggering over the course of a career.

That is why this book is so timely and so needed.

Tax Efficient White Coat brings clarity to an area that has long been overlooked and misunderstood. Paavan and the DFO team shine a light on what is possible when you move from passive compliance to intentional tax strategy. They simplify complex concepts into actionable steps that empower you to protect your income, reduce your tax burden, and build long-term wealth with confidence.

For practice owners especially, your greatest opportunity for growth is often found inside your own business. Careful tax strategy can free up the capital you need to reinvest—whether that's adding an operatory, upgrading technology, hiring talent, or launching a second location. The right tax plan doesn't just save money—it fuels expansion, elevates patient care, and accelerates your path to financial freedom.

This book is more than education—it's a mindset shift. A roadmap to move from "tax happens to me" to "I control my tax outcome." Whether you are early in your career, building a thriving practice, or planning your exit, the insights here will equip you to approach your financial life with the same preventative care philosophy you apply every day in your profession.

You care deeply for your patients. It's time to care just as intentionally for the wealth your hard work creates.

I am honored to introduce this book, and I hope it is a turning point in how you approach your financial journey going forward.

— **Michelle Lafrinere, CPA**
Director of Tax, Pro-Fi 20/20 Dental CPAs
Partner, Phase One Dental CPAs

WHO SHOULD READ THIS BOOK?

This book is for you if you're:

- An employed dentist (DDS/DMD), medical doctor (MD/DO), veterinarian (DVM) or another high-income healthcare professional earning $300,000+ and watching 35-45% disappear to taxes every year
- A practice owner or partner generating significant revenue but feeling like you're on a hamster wheel
- A specialist (cardiologists, anesthesiologists, radiologists, orthopedic surgeons, neurosurgeons, oral & maxillofacial surgeons, dental specialists, veterinary surgeon etc.) approaching partnership and trying to understand the financial implications
- A resident or fellow planning ahead and wanting to avoid the financial mistakes most doctors make wants to keep more of what you earn

You spent over a decade learning medicine. This book will teach you what they didn't cover in medical, dental, or veterinarian school: how to stop the financial bleeding and build real wealth.

MY PROMISE TO YOU

I won't waste your time.

You're busy. You work 50-70 hour weeks. You have patients to see, families to support, and lives to save. The last thing you need is another 300-page book full of theory and jargon.

As Oliver Wendell Holmes Jr. once said, *"For the simplicity that lies this side of complexity, I would not give a fig; but for the simplicity that lies on the other side of complexity, I would give my life."*

My hope is that, after reading this book, you arrive at that **profound simplicity**—the kind that emerges only after navigating complexity with clarity and intention.

COMPLEXITY

SIMPLICITY

PROFOUND SIMPLICITY

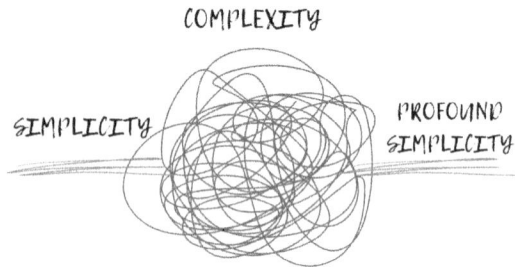

So here's my promise:

Every strategy in this book is practical, compliant, and built to be implemented in the real world. I'm not going to tell you about exotic offshore tax shelters or sketchy loopholes. I'm going to show you the same strategies that billionaires and ultra-high-net-worth families have used for decades adapted specifically for high-income dentists, doctors, and vets.

Every chapter will end with action steps. No vague advice. No "consult with a professional and maybe something good will happen." You'll know exactly what to do next.

To make the world of tax from confounding to profound simplicity. I'll explain complex concepts in plain English. No unnecessary jargon. No 80-page explanations of minutiae. I'll try to use medical analogies and lingo were relavant. If you can understand a patient's chart, you can understand these strategies.

You'll see yourself in these stories. Every example in this book is based on real doctors I've worked with over the past two decades. The names and details have been changed, but the challenges, frustrations, and breakthroughs are real.

By the end of this book, you'll understand:

- Why you're paying so much in taxes (and how to fix it)
- The three pillars every tax strategy is built on
- How to save $50,000-$200,000+ per year in taxes
- How to hire a coordinated team that works for you (not just hire a hodgepodge or disconnected advisors)
- How to turn your medical career into generational wealth

I won't be repeating any financial concepts I introduced in *"Effortless Wealth: The S.W.A.N.™ Approach to Unlocking Wealth for* **Busy Professionals".** If you are interested in learning those concepts I recommend you read that book. It's a very simple read, quicker than this book, but has some foundational financial concepts.

Most importantly, you'll learn how to **Sleep Well At Night (S.W.A.N.™)**—the guiding principle of everything I do.

Let's get started.

PROLOGUE: THE DAY A SLEEPING MONKEY GOT THE BEST OF ME

❦

*S*ometimes purpose doesn't change, only the way you practice it. —
Paavan Kotini

THE MONKEY WAS SEDATED.

I was supposed to be calm, focused, and steady —everything a
future oncologist needed to be. It was just another day in the lab at
Vanderbilt University Medical Center, where I spent years
researching cancer, dreaming of the day I'd wear a white coat and save
lives.

But then I nicked a vein.

Blood spurted everywhere-bright, urgent, impossible to ignore.
The room tilted. My vision tunneled. And the next thing I knew, I was
flat on my back, staring up at fluorescent lights while six scientists
stood over me, faces twisted in a mixture of concern and... was that
amusement?

"Do we help Paavan or save the monkey?" someone asked.

Five of them chose the monkey.

I can't blame them, really. That monkey was worth more to the
research than my bruised ego. The junior scientist, bless him—

1

dragged me out by my feet, propped them up, and threw water on my face until I came to.

This wasn't the first time it had happened. And it wouldn't be the last.

I had a problem: I had a vasovagal response meaning I couldn't see blood without passing out. Which, as you might imagine, is a fairly significant obstacle when you're planning to become a doctor. There goes my future in medicine.

* * *

THE PATH I Thought I'd Take

My name is Paavan Kotini, and I was never supposed to end up in finance.

I was supposed to be an oncologist.

From my high school evenings and weekends at the Medical College of Virginia to my years as a biomedical engineer at Vanderbilt University, I was immersed in cancer research, studying ways to heal people. I had a theory, one that bridged ancient wisdom and modern science.

Growing up around Ayurvedic traditions, I was fascinated by Neem, a tree revered in India for its remarkable healing properties. During my research years, that fascination evolved into a scientific pursuit. Neem leaves contain a range of bioactive compounds, and I had identified one in particular, Azadirachtin A, a limonoid molecule that I believed might influence the behavior of cancer cells.

To me, it represented a bridge between centuries-old natural medicine and cutting-edge oncology research. At the time, I wasn't just experimenting; it felt like purpose taking shape, an attempt to prove that healing could be both ancient and innovative at once.

I was convinced that was my life's purpose. But life had other plans. It has a way of rerouting purpose. I just didn't realize then that one day, I'd still be helping people stop the bleeding-only this time, the kind measured in time, effort and dollars, not drops.

* * *

THE PIVOT

After that incident with the monkey, I had to face an uncomfortable truth: I couldn't pursue medicine. Not if I couldn't handle the sight of blood. So I did what any good South Asian kid does when they can't be a doctor, I pivoted to technology.

I ended up at Apple, working on the first iPhone project. It was exciting, innovative, a complete departure from the lab. But it wasn't medicine. It wasn't healing. And I felt... lost.

Then came the moment that changed everything.

I was filling out my 401(k) paperwork-you know, that stack of forms HR gives you on your first day that you're supposed to understand but nobody actually explains. I stared at the investment options: large-cap growth, small-cap value, international equity, bond funds. It was like reading a foreign language.

So I did what anyone would do: I asked my friends.

"What did you pick?" I asked one colleague.

"Oh, I just chose whatever he chose," he said, pointing to another coworker.

"And what did you pick?" I asked that coworker.

"I just chose the default. Seemed easy."

This couldn't be right. This couldn't be how successful, intelligent people built wealth. We were engineers at one of the most innovative companies in the world, and we were making retirement decisions based on... what? Convenience? Guesswork? Whatever the person next to us did?

* * *

THE DISCOVERY

I decided to ask someone who actually knew what they were doing (or so I thought): my father.

My dad had helped build the technology team at Capital One and left as an executive in 2002. After that, he became an entrepreneur, building several successful businesses. If anyone knew about money, it was him.

"Dad," I said, "can you help me understand this 401(k) stuff? And while we're at it, can you show me how you've structured your finances? I want to learn."

He laughed-not unkindly, but with the weariness of someone who'd been too busy building to stop and organize.

"Paavan," he said, "I know how to earn money. I know how to save money. But I'm too busy to figure out what to do after that. But you're welcome to look under the hood."

So I did.

And what I found shocked me.

Without any formal training in finance, even I could see it was a mess. Disjointed investments. Overlapping insurance policies. Tax strategies that weren't strategies at all-just reactions. For someone as successful as my father, far too much was being lost to bad investments, excessive taxes, and financial inefficiency.

It didn't make sense to him. It didn't make sense to me. But more importantly, it didn't seem right.

That's when I got curious.

* * *

The New Mission

In 2007, I made a decision that would change my life: I entered the financial industry. Not because I wanted a career in finance-I didn't. I did it to learn. To help my parents. To help myself. To help a few family friends who were in the same boat.

But as I dove deeper, I discovered something that made my blood boil (ironically, the only blood that didn't make me pass out): there were tools, strategies, and structures that billionaires and ultra-high-net-worth families had access to that regular high-income earners-doctors, engineers, business owners-had no idea even existed.

Why? Because nobody was teaching them. Nobody was showing

them. The financial industry was built to sell products, not to plan proactively.

Then 2008 happened.

The market crashed. Lehman Brothers collapsed. Panic spread like wildfire. Financial advisors were leaving the industry in droves, and clients were losing fortunes.

But the families I'd been working with? Most of them were protected. Some even grew their wealth during the downturn because we'd planned ahead, structured things properly, and didn't panic.

"Paavan, can you help my brother?" one client asked.

"Can you help my sister?" asked another.

"Why aren't you doing this full-time?"

That's when I had my epiphany.

I'd gotten into medicine because I wanted to help people. I thought the only way to do that was by becoming a doctor. But here I was, making a real, tangible impact on people's lives-not by stopping physical bleeding, but by stopping financial bleeding.

The mission hadn't changed. Only the method had.

* * *

BUILDING KOTINI & Kotini

So while everyone else was running away from the financial industry, I doubled down. I went all in. I built a firm-Kotini & Kotini-evolved over two decades of work and designed specifically for first-generation wealth builders: the doctors, dentists, engineers, and entrepreneurs who earn great incomes but don't come from generational wealth, who don't have family offices or trust fund advisors, who are building everything from scratch.

We created what we call the DFO - Doctor's or Dentist's Family Office - a multidisciplinary team approach inspired by the very thing I'd studied for years: medicine.

In medicine, you don't treat a patient in isolation. You have specialists. You have rounds. You have a team that communicates, coordinates, and collaborates to create the best outcome.

Why shouldn't your finances work the same way?

That's what this book is about.

* * *

THE FULL CIRCLE

Fast forward nearly twenty years from when I got into the financial industry, and I've had the privilege of working with hundreds of physicians, dentists, and high-income professionals. I've seen the same patterns over and over again:

Brilliant people who save lives, build businesses, and serve their communities... but who are getting destroyed by taxes.

Doctors who earn $500,000 a year but feel broke.

Specialists who work 80-hour weeks but can't seem to get ahead.

Practice owners who generate millions in revenue but watch half of it disappear to Uncle Sam.

And here's the tragedy: it doesn't have to be this way.

The strategies in this book aren't theoretical. They're not reserved for billionaires. They're practical, legal, and ethical ways that dentists, doctors and vets —yes, even W-2 employed —can reduce their tax burden, build real wealth, and create the financial freedom they've earned.

I may not have gone on to treat patients as a medical doctor and stop physical bleeding, but I found my own kind of triage-helping people like you stop the financial bleeding.

And that's exactly what we're going to do.

PART I
THE DIAGNOSIS

YOU CAN'T TREAT WHAT YOU HAVEN'T
MEASURED

This section uncovers financial blind spots—helping you read your 1040 like a radiologist and spot where wealth is silently bleeding out.

CHAPTER 1

THE BIG LIE IN THE WHITE COAT

"It's not how much money you make, but how much you keep, how hard it works for you, and how many generations you keep it for." —Robert Kiyosaki

"Income doesn't equal wealth any more than a heartbeat equals health." — *Paavan Kotini*

1. THE BIG LIE IN THE WHITE COAT

*et me start with a question that might sting a little:
      How much of your income did you lose to taxes last year?

Go ahead. Pull up your tax return. Look at line 24 on your Form 1040 —that's your total tax (Refer to Appendix B for more understanding of the 1040). Now divide that by your gross income.

What's the percentage?

If you're a physician earning $300,000 to $500,000 a year, you're probably looking at an effective federal tax rate of 25% to 35%. Add in state taxes (depending on where you live), and you're easily pushing 35% to 45% total.

Let's make this concrete. If you're a hospitalist earning $350,000 a year and you're paying 40% in combined federal and state taxes, you're sending $140,000 to the government. Every. Single. Year.

Over a 30-year career, that's $4.2 million in taxes.

Read that again: **$4.2 million.**

Now let me ask you another question: **What's your single largest lifetime expense?**

Most doctors say their house. Maybe their kids' education. Some say their student loans.

They're all wrong.

Your single largest lifetime expense-by far-is taxes.

Not your mortgage. Not your car. Not even your malpractice insurance.

Taxes.

And yet, when was the last time someone taught you how to plan for them?

The Big Lie

In medical school, you learned anatomy, pharmacology, pathology. You did rotations. You studied for boards. You trained for years to become an expert in your field.

But nobody taught you about tax planning, which is different from tax filing (we'll get more into the difference later). Nobody explained the difference between W-2 income and business income. Nobody showed you how depreciation works, or what a cost segregation study is, or how to structure entities to protect and grow wealth.

You were taught to earn. But not to keep.

And that's the big lie in the white coat: **High income equals wealth.**

It doesn't.

Wealth isn't what you earn. Wealth is what you keep after taxes, after expenses, after inflation, after life happens.

And if you're not proactively planning your taxes, you're not building wealth-you're just funding the government's budget.

* * *

ESTIMATED Lifetime Federal Tax by Physician Specialty

Here's what most doctors will pay in federal taxes alone over a 30-year career:

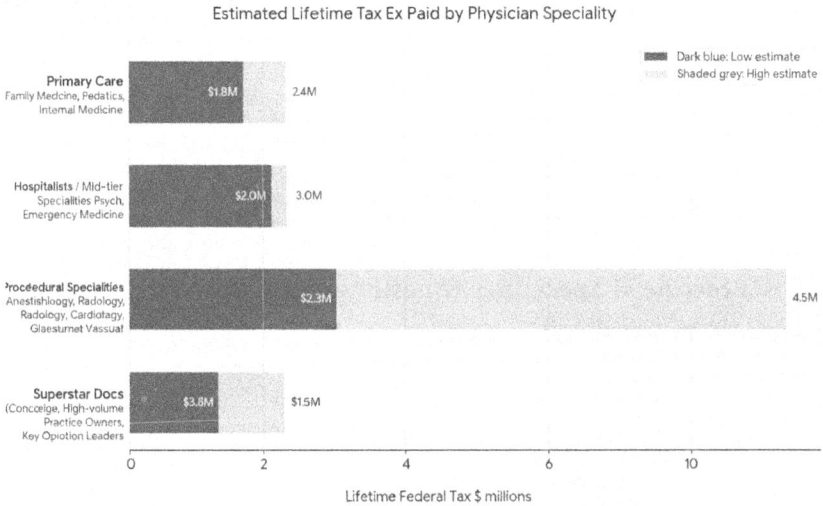

Figure 1.1: Estimated Lifetime Federal Tax Paid by Physician Specialty in $ Millions. Dark blue is the low estimate, and the shaded grey is the high estimate.

Assumptions:

- Career span: 30 years (post-residency)
- Average annual income source: Medscape 2024 + American Medical Association (AMA) compensation surveys (2024)
- Effective federal tax rate: 25-30% (depending on deductions, planning, family status)
- Excludes state taxes, payroll taxes, and NIIT— these would add another 20-40% on top

1. Primary Care (Family Medicine, Pediatrics, Internal Medicine)

- Avg income: $230k-$270k
- Lifetime income: ~$7M-$8M
- **Lifetime federal tax: $1.8M-$2.4M**

2. Hospitalists / Mid-tier Specialties (Psych, Neurology, Emergency Medicine)

- Avg income: $300k-$350k
- Lifetime income: ~$9M-$10M
- **Lifetime federal tax: $2.3M-$3M**

3. Procedural Specialties (Anesthesiology, Radiology, Cardiology, Gastroenterology)

- Avg income: $400k-$500k
- Lifetime income: ~$12M-$15M
- **Lifetime federal tax: $3M-$4.5M**

4. Surgical Specialties (Orthopedics, Neurosurgery, Plastic, Vascular)

- Avg income: $600k-$800k (some over $1M)
- Lifetime income: ~$18M-$25M
- **Lifetime federal tax: $4.5M-$7.5M**

5. "Superstar Docs" (Concierge, High-volume Practice Owners, Key Opinion Leaders)

- Avg income: $1M+
- Lifetime income: $30M+
- **Lifetime federal tax: $7.5M-$10M+**

* * *

ESTIMATED Lifetime Federal Tax by Dentist Category

Here's what most dentist's will pay in federal taxes alone over a 30-year career:

Estimated Lifetime Federal Tax Paid by Dentist Category ($ millions)

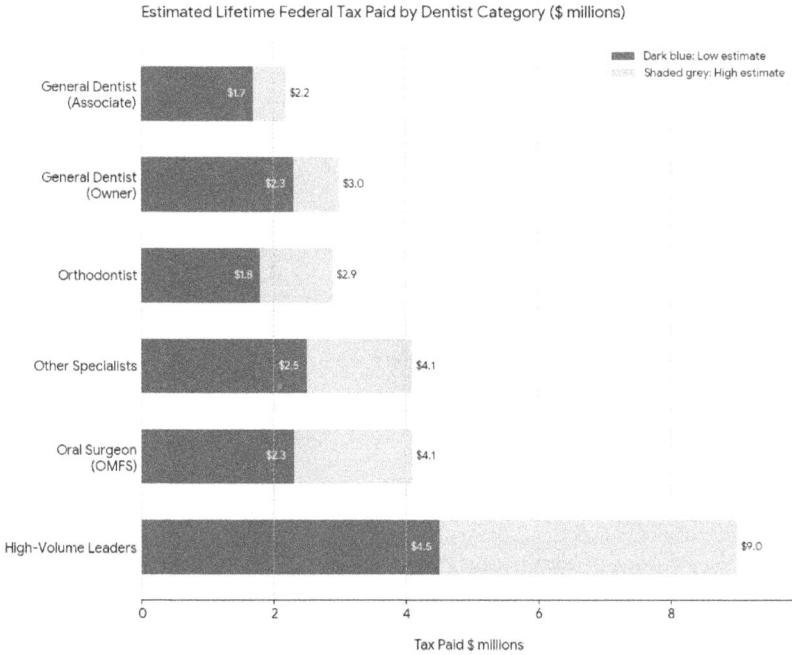

Figure 1.2: Estimated Lifetime Federal Tax Paid by Dentist Category in $ millions. Dark blue is the low estimate, and shaded grey is the high estimate. Sources: ADA Health Policy Institute (2024), DentalPost Salary Survey (2024–2025), BLS Specialist Data (2024).

ASSUMPTIONS

- Career span: 30 years (post-residency or full-practice)
- Average annual income sources: ADA Health Policy Institute 2024 Survey of Dental Practice and recent national surveys
- Effective federal tax rate: 25–30% (planning, filing status, deductions)
- Excludes state taxes, payroll taxes, and NIIT, which could add ~20–40% on top

1. General Dentist —Employed Associate

- Avg income: $225k–$245k
- Lifetime income: ~$6.8M–$7.4M
- Lifetime federal tax (25–30%): $1.7M–$2.2M

2. General Dentist —Practice Owner/Partner

- Avg income: ~$300k–$330k
- Lifetime income: ~$9.0M–$9.9M
- Lifetime federal tax: $2.3M–$3.0M

3. Orthodontist

- Avg income: ~$240k–$325k+
- Lifetime income: ~$7.2M–$9.8M
- Lifetime federal tax: $1.8M–$2.9M

4. Endodontist / Periodontist / Prosthodontist

- Avg income: ~$325k–$450k
- Lifetime income: ~$9.8M–$13.5M
- Lifetime federal tax: $2.5M–$4.1M

5. Oral & Maxillofacial Surgeon (OMFS)

- Avg income: ~$310k–$450k+
- Lifetime income: ~$9.3M–$13.5M+
- Lifetime federal tax: $2.3M–$4.1M+

6. High-Volume Owners / DSO Leaders / Key Opinion Leaders

- Avg income: ~$600k–$1.0M+
- Lifetime income: ~$18M–$30M+
- Lifetime federal tax: $4.5M–$9.0M+

* * *

ESTIMATED Lifetime Federal Tax by Veterinarian Category

Here's what most Veterinarian's will pay in federal taxes alone over a 30-year career:

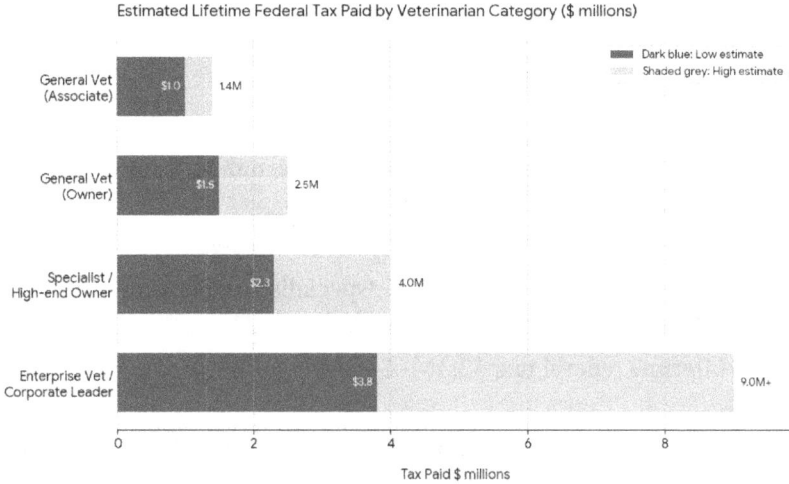

Figure 1.3: Estimated Lifetime Federal Tax Paid by Veterinarian Category in $ millions. Dark blue is the low estimate, and the shaded grey is the high estimate. Sources: American Veterinary Medical Association (AVMA) industry discussion, Bureau of Labor Statistics (2024 median & range)

Assumptions:

- Career span: 30 years (post-residency or full-practice)
- Average annual income sources: BLS median + industry specialty/ownership premiums
- Effective federal tax rate: 25-30% (planning, filing status, deductions)
- Excludes state taxes, payroll taxes, and NIIT, which could add ~20-40% on top

1. General Veterinarian —Employed Associate

- Avg income: ~$130k–$160k
- Lifetime income: ~$3.9M–$4.8M
- Lifetime federal tax (25–30%): $1.0M–$1.4M

2. General Veterinarian —Practise Owner/ Partner

- Avg income: ~$200k–$275k (ownership premium)
- Lifetime income: ~$6.0M–$8.3M
- Lifetime federal tax: $1.5M–$2.5M

3. Veterinary Specialist —(Surgery, Internal Medicine, referral) / high-end owner

- Avg income: ~$300k–$450k+ (specialist/owner premium)
- Lifetime income: ~$9.0M–$13.5M
- Lifetime federal tax: $2.3M–$4.0M

4. Enterprise Veterinarian/ Multi-site owner/ Key Opinion Leader/ Corporate Vet Leader

- Avg income: ~$500k–$1.0M+
- Lifetime income: ~$15.0M–$30.0M+
- Lifetime federal tax: $3.8M–$9.0M+

* * *

THE W-2 TRAP

Let's talk about the W-2 trap, because this is where most employed physicians get stuck.

When you're a W-2 employee-whether you're working for a hospital, a large group, private practice, or an academic institution-your income is reported on a W-2 form. Your employer withholds taxes from every paycheck. And at the end of the year, you file your tax return, maybe get a small refund (which is just your own money being returned to you, by the way), and you move on.

Here's the problem: **W-2 income is the highest-taxed income in America.**

It's taxed as ordinary income, which means you're paying the top marginal rates. In 2024, if you're married filing jointly and earning over $364,200, you're in the 35% federal bracket. Earn over $731,200, and you're in the 37% bracket.

Add in state taxes-10% in California, 13.3% if you're really successful-and you're losing nearly half of every dollar you earn.

But here's what most doctors don't realize: **the tax code isn't designed to punish you. It's designed to incentivize certain behaviors.**

The government wants you to:

- Invest in real estate (depreciation deductions)
- Start businesses (business expense deductions)
- Save for retirement (401(k) and defined benefit plan contributions)
- Invest in renewable energy (solar tax credits)
- Preserve historic properties (historic tax credits)

The tax code is full of legal, ethical ways to reduce your tax burden-but only if you know they exist and only if you plan for them proactively.

W-2 employees don't get those opportunities beyond 401(k) automatically. You have to create them.

And that's what this book is going to teach you.

* * *

THE CURRENT ECONOMIC Reality

But doctors aren't just fighting their own tax bill-they're fighting against the backdrop of a national balance sheet that's fundamentally unsustainable.

* * *

The U.S. Debt Crisis

The United States currently carries **$38+ trillion in national debt** (and growing). Interest payments alone are now the **single largest line item** in the federal budget-surpassing defense spending.

That means more of your future tax dollars will go not toward building, but toward **servicing old promises.**

* * *

Rising Tax Scenarios

Historically, the U.S. top marginal tax rate has been as high as **94% (1944-45)** and stayed above **70% for decades.** Today's top rate (37%) is historically *low*-but with debt and deficits rising, it's highly likely dentists, physicians and vets in their 30s, 40s, and 50s will see **significantly higher tax rates in their peak earning years.**

Translation: doctors are walking into the crosshairs.

Figure 1.4: Highest U.S. Federal Marginal Income Tax Rate, 1913 – 2025. The top individual income tax rate has ranged from 7% in 1913 to 94% during World War II, reflecting shifts in fiscal policy, wartime funding, and major reform acts such as the 1964 Revenue Act, the Tax Reform Act of 1986, and the Tax Cuts and Jobs Act (TCJA 2017). Vertical shaded bands denote key legislative eras that reshaped U.S. tax policy. Sources: U.S. Internal Revenue Code historical tables; Urban-Brookings Tax Policy Center ("Historical Highest Marginal Income Tax Rates, 1913–2015"); Tax Foundation and NTU Foundation updates for 2016–2025 (TCJA period)

* * *

How the Government **Makes Returns**

Governments don't sell products. They collect revenue almost entirely through **taxation and inflation.**

- **Taxes:** The most direct tool-raise brackets, eliminate deductions, phase out credits
- **Inflation:** A hidden tax-erodes the value of your dollar without an act of Congress
- The IRS is the collection arm, and **W-2 earners are the easiest targets** because taxes are withheld automatically (I in IRS is for Income tax based on <u>taxable</u> income. Taxable being the key).

* * *

What This Means **for Doctors**

High, stable incomes make you the IRS's "perfect customer." Rising debt + rising healthcare costs + entitlement obligations (Social Security, Medicare) = doctors will almost certainly shoulder a larger share in the future.

Without proactive planning, you're on track to not only fund your own family's future, but also the government's balance sheet.

The Filer vs. The Planner

There are two types of doctors when it comes to taxes: **The Filer** and **The Planner.**

The Filer does their taxes once a year, usually in March or April. They hand their documents to their CPA, who plugs numbers into software, files the return, and sends them a bill. The Filer pays whatever the tax software says they owe. They might complain about it, but they don't question it. They assume that's just how it works.

The Planner, on the other hand, thinks about taxes year-round. They meet with their CPA or family office in Q1 to set goals. They make strategic decisions throughout the year: when to make purchases, how to structure income, where to invest. They ask questions. They explore options. And when April comes around, they're not surprised by their tax bill, because they've been planning for it all along.

Here's the difference in results:

The Filer pays whatever they're told to pay.

The Planner pays the **legal** minimum.

Over a 30-year career, that difference can be millions of dollars.

Let me say that again: **millions of dollars.**

Not because the Planner is doing anything shady or illegal. But because they're using the tools the tax code provides —tools that the Filer doesn't even know exist.

* * *

Why Your CPA Might Be Part of the Problem

Now, before we go any further, I need to address something uncomfortable: your CPA might not be helping you the way you think they are.

I'm not saying your CPA is bad at their job. Most CPAs are smart, hardworking, ethical professionals. But here's the issue: **most CPAs are trained to be historians, not strategists.**

The tax code is 80,000+ pages, and Google has 875,000,000 results when you search "Tax Planning," yet only a fraction of tax planning is actually happening vs. tax filing. No way that any one CPA can know all 80,000+ pages of IRS tax code— it requires a team!

Moreover, they're trained to look backward-to take last year's numbers, categorize them, and file your return accurately and on time. That's reactive compliance. And compliance is important.

But compliance is **not** planning.

Planning is forward-looking. Planning is proactive. Planning is asking, "What can we do differently this year to reduce your tax burden next year?"

And most CPAs don't do that-not because they don't care, but because they're not structured to do it. They're busy. They have hundreds of clients. And they get paid to file returns, not to strategize.

So here's what happens: You go to your CPA in March with a box of receipts. They enter your W-2, your mortgage interest, your student loan interest, maybe your HSA contribution. They run the numbers. You owe $80,000. You write the check. You leave.

And nobody ever asks: **"Could we have done this differently?"**

That's the gap this book is designed to fill.

* * *

QUESTIONS TO THINK About

Before we move on, I want you to sit with these questions. Don't rush past them. Really think about your answers.

1. **How much of your income did you lose to taxes last year?** *(If you don't know, go find out. Pull up your tax return right now.)*
2. **Did you take the standard deduction, or did you itemize?** *(If you're not sure, pull up last year's return and find out. And if you did itemize, look closely at how much of that deduction you actually used.)*
3. **If taxes are your single largest lifetime expense, why haven't you been trained to plan for them?** *(Seriously—why is this not part of medical school? Why is this not part of residency?)*
4. **Are you a Filer or a Planner?** *(Be honest. When was the last time you had a proactive tax planning conversation with your CPA?)*

* * *

QUESTIONS TO ASK Your CPA

The next time you meet with your CPA, ask them these questions. Their answers will tell you everything you need to know about whether you're working with a historian or a strategist.

1. **Am I just filing, or are we proactively planning my taxes?**

If they say, "Well, we file your return every year and make sure it's accurate," that's a red flag. That's **compliance**, *not* **planning**. *It's the difference between someone working for the IRS and someone working for you.*

If they say, "We meet quarterly to review your income, discuss upcoming expenses, and explore strategies to reduce your tax burden," that's a potential green flag. That's planning. That could be a good start.

1. **What are 2-3 ways we could reduce my effective tax rate this year?**

If they can't immediately give you specific, actionable strategies, that's a problem. A good CPA should have a mental rolodex of strategies based on your situation.

1. **"Can you show me my effective tax rate over the last 5 years? Where do I rank compared to other physicians you work with?"**

This question does two things: First, it shows you whether your CPA is tracking your progress over time. Second, it shows you whether they're benchmarking you against peers.

If your effective tax rate is 35% and other physicians they work with are at 25%, you need to know why. What are they doing that you're not?

* * *

THE BOTTOM LINE

Here's the truth: **You didn't go to medical school to become a tax expert. But you can't afford to ignore taxes.**

You spent years learning how to diagnose and treat patients. You can spend a few hours learning how to diagnose and treat your tax situation.

Because here's what I've learned after nearly two decades in this industry: **The doctors who build real wealth aren't the ones who earn the most. They're the ones who keep the most.**

And keeping more starts with understanding the big lie: high income does not equal wealth.

Wealth is what's left after taxes.

So let's stop the bleeding.

CHAPTER 2

❧

THE JOURNEY OF TWO DOCS

"A goal without a plan is just a wish." —Antoine de Saint-Exupéry

"The difference between the filer and the planner isn't intelligence-it's intention." —Paavan Kotini

2. THE JOURNEY OF TWO DOCS

*L*et me introduce you to two doctors.

They graduated from the same medical school. They completed residency in the same year. They both became hospitalists at reputable institutions. They both earn **$350,000 a year.**

On paper, they're identical.

Thirty years later, one retires with **$8 million in net worth.** The other retires with **$3 million.**

Same income. Same career. **$5 million difference.**

How?

Let me tell you their stories.

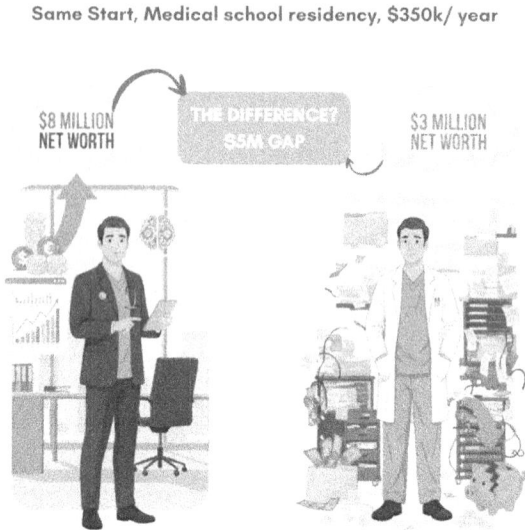

Same Start, Medical school residency, $350k/ year

$8 MILLION NET WORTH

THE DIFFERENCE? $5M GAP

$3 MILLION NET WORTH

Figure 2.1: Same income. Same career. Two Mindsets. **$5 million difference.** Which one are you? Or better, which do you want to be?

Meet Dr. Michael Anderson: The Filer

Dr. Michael Anderson is a good doctor. His patients love him. His colleagues respect him.

He works hard, saves diligently, and "does all the right things."

He maxes out his **401(k)** every year — **$23,500 in 2025 (or $31,000 if he's over 50)**.

He contributes to his **HSA — $4,300 (individual)** or **$8,550 (family)** in 2025.

He pays his bills on time. He invests in a standard portfolio of index funds.

Every April, Michael gathers his tax documents — W-2, mortgage interest statement, 1099s — and drops them off at his CPA's office. Two weeks later, he gets the call:

"You owe $95,000 in federal and state taxes."

He sighs, writes the check, and assumes that's just the cost of success.

Year after year, the pattern repeats.

Income: $350,000

Taxes: ~$95,000 (≈27% effective rate)

Savings: 401(k), brokerage, and hope the markets cooperate.

He retires with **about $3 million**, mostly in tax-deferred accounts. Not bad — but not great either.

Meet Dr. Arjun Mehta: The Planner

Dr. Arjun Mehta earns the same $350,000.

But he approaches money differently.

In his first year out of residency, he didn't just find a CPA — he found a **proactive tax planner** who met with him in Q1 to ask,

"What can we do this year to reduce next year's taxes?"

He also built a small "family office" of professionals — a CPA, financial advisor, attorney, and insurance strategist — who communicated with each other.

* * *

YEARS 1–5: Laying the Foundation

Arjun maxed out his **401(k)** — $23,500 (or $31,000 if over 50).

He opened a **backdoor Roth IRA** and contributed **$7,000 per year** (growing tax-free forever).

He also opened an **LLC** for medical consulting and speaking income (~$20,000 a year), allowing deductions for home-office expenses, CME travel, and professional development — saving about **$5,000** annually in taxes.

He bought a small rental property and worked with his CPA to complete a **cost segregation study**, accelerating depreciation and creating a **$40,000 deduction** in Year 1 — another **$14,000 in tax savings.**

Total Year 1 savings: ~$19,000 vs. Dr. Anderson.

* * *

YEARS 6–15: Building Momentum

Arjun bought a second property and repeated the cost segregation strategy.

He installed a **solar system** using the 30% federal **Clean Energy Credit (OBBBA)** — saving **$15,000** on a $50,000 installation.

He added a **Cash Balance Plan** through his consulting LLC, deferring an additional **$100,000+ per year** on top of his 401(k). That alone saved **$35,000–$40,000 per year** in taxes.

He funded an **Indexed Universal Life (IUL)** policy, contributing **$30,000 annually** for long-term, tax-free cash value accumulation.

Annual tax savings during this phase: ≈ $50,000.

* * *

YEARS 16–30: Mastering the Multiplier

Arjun's rental portfolio appreciated.

He executed **1031 exchanges** to defer capital gains taxes while upgrading assets.

He formed an **831(b) micro-captive insurance company** for his consulting business — deducting up to **$2.5 million annually** while building a reserve asset.

He also implemented **Leveraged Charitable Donations**, turning **$50,000 of cash into $250,000 of deductions** by donating appreciated assets through a charitable LLC.

Tax savings during this phase: ≈ $75,000+ per year.

The 30-Year Math

	Dr. Anderson (The Filer)	Dr. Mehta (The Planner)
Total Career Earnings	$10.5 M	$10.5 M
Taxes Paid	$2.85 M (27%)	$1.65 M (15.7%)
Total Invested After Tax	$3.0 M	$4.2 M
Net Worth at Retirement	$3 M	$8 M

Figure 2.2: The 30 year math. Same income. Same career. **$5 million difference.** The secret wasn't luck — it was intention.

* * *

THE POWER of Small Wins

You don't have to cut your tax bill in half overnight.

Small, consistent wins compound.

- A **$5,000 annual tax savings** grows to ~$472,000 over 30 years (7% growth).

- A **$20,000 annual tax savings** grows to ~$1.89 million.

- A **$50,000 annual tax savings** grows to ~$4.72 million.

You don't need to slice your tax bill in half overnight.

Small wins stack. That's the quiet magic of proactive planning.

Consistent wins snowball.

And over 30 years, tax savings invested well can quietly turn into millions.

* * *

CLINICAL SCAN: **The Two Paths Diverge**

Let's look at a specific year to see how their paths diverged.

	Dr. Michael Anderson	Dr. Arjun Mehta
Income	$350,000	$400,000 (includes consulting)
401(k)	– $23,500	– $23,500
HSA	– $8,550	– $8,550
Cash Balance Plan	—	– $100,000
Home Office / Business Expenses	—	– $15,000
Rental Depreciation (Cost-Seg)	—	– $60,000
Standard Deduction	– $29,200	—
Total Deductions	– $61,250	– $207,050
Taxable Income	$288,750	$192,950
Tax (Fed + State)	≈ $95,000	≈ $65,000
Solar Credit	—	– $15,000
Total Tax	$95,000	$50,000
Effective Rate	27%	12.5%
Tax Savings (Year 10)	—	$45,000

Figure 2.3: Two paths diverge in Tax Strategy (Year 10)

Dr. Mehta didn't evade taxes — he **orchestrated** them.

He used what the tax code *intentionally rewards*: business owner-ship, energy investment, retirement deferral, and strategic giving.

* * *

THE LESSON

Dr. Anderson worked hard *in* his career.

Dr. Mehta worked hard *on* his financial structure.

Over time, that difference turned compliance into compounding.

Small wins, applied deliberately, transformed his wealth — and his ability to **Sleep Well At Night.**

* * *

WHICH DOCTOR ARE YOU?

So here's the question: **Which doctor do you relate to more right now?**

Are you Michael-working hard, earning well, but watching a huge chunk of your income disappear to taxes every year without questioning it?

Or are you Arjun-proactively planning, asking questions, exploring strategies, and building a team to help you keep more of what you earn?

If you're Michael right now, that's okay. Most doctors are. But the good news is, you don't have to stay Michael.

You can become Arjun. Starting today.

* * *

QUESTIONS TO THINK About

1. **Which doctor do you relate to more right now-Michael or Arjun?** (*Be honest. There's no judgment here. Awareness is the first step.*)
2. **If your future self looked back 30 years from now, what would you regret more: paying too much in taxes, or missing the chance to plan?** (*Think about that. Really think about it.*)

3. **What's one small win you could implement this year that would save you $5,000, $10,000, or $20,000 in taxes?** *(We'll explore specific strategies in the coming chapters, but start thinking about it now.)*

* * *

Questions to Ask Your CPA

The next time you meet with your CPA, ask them these questions:

1. **Can you show me my effective tax rate over the last 5 years?** *(This will show you whether your tax burden is going up, down, or staying flat. If it's going up (or staying flat at a high rate), that's a red flag.)*
2. **Where do I rank compared to other physicians you work with?** *(If your CPA works with other doctors, they should be able to tell you (in general terms) how your effective tax rate compares. If you're paying 30% and others are paying 20%, you need to know why.)*
3. **What's one strategy we could implement this year to reduce my effective tax rate?** *(A good CPA should be able to give you at least one actionable idea. If they can't, it might be time to find a new CPA.)*

* * *

The Bottom Line

The difference between Michael and Arjun isn't intelligence. It's not work ethic. It's not even income.

The difference is **intentionality.**

Michael reacted. Arjun planned.

Michael filed. Arjun strategized.

Michael hoped. Arjun executed.

And over 30 years, that made a $5 million difference.

So here's my challenge to you: **Stop being Michael. Start being Arjun.**

You've earned your income. Now let's make sure you keep it.

PART II
THE ART OF TAX PLANNING

MICRO STRATEGIES FOR THE NOW

This is where tactical tax moves—deductions, depreciation, and deferrals—become your instruments for immediate relief and long-term leverage.

CHAPTER 3

❧

THE THREE PILLARS OF TAX PLANNING

"Plans are nothing; planning is everything." —*Dwight D. Eisenhower*

"Tax planning isn't about loopholes-it's about alignment: your goals, your numbers, your future." —*Paavan Kotini*

THE THREE PILLARS OF TAX PLANNING

❧

*B*efore we dive into specific strategies, we need to establish a framework. Think of this as your diagnostic tool-a way to evaluate every tax strategy you encounter and determine whether it's right for you.

There are three pillars of tax planning:

1. **Deductions** (reduce your taxable income)
2. **Credits** (reduce your tax bill dollar-for-dollar)
3. **Depreciation** (accelerate deductions on assets)

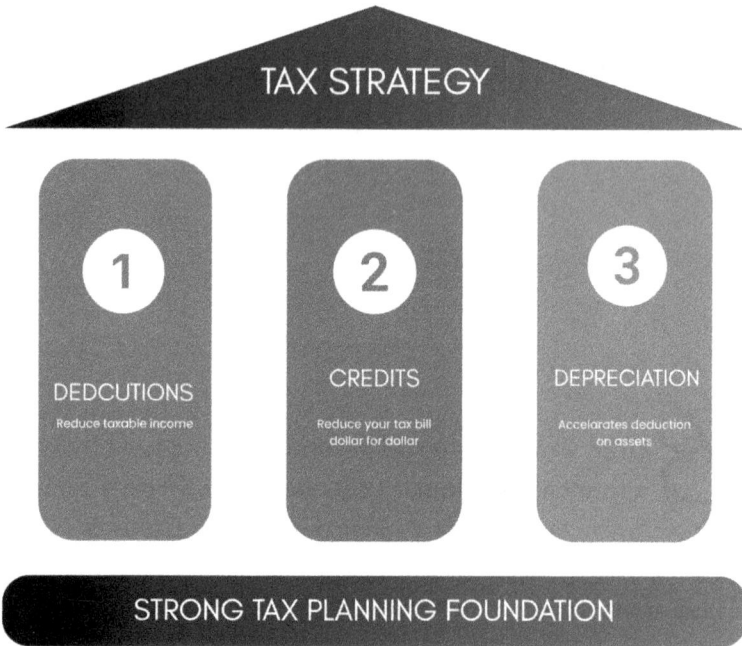

Figure 3.1: Almost every tax strategy you'll ever encounter falls into one of these three categories, hence, we call them the three pillars of tax planning.

Almost every tax strategy you'll ever encounter falls into one of these three categories. Master these, and you'll have a lens through which to evaluate every opportunity that comes your way.

Let's break them down.

* * *

Pillar 1: Deductions

A deduction reduces your taxable income.

Here's how it works: Let's say you earn $350,000 and you're in the 35% federal tax bracket. If you can deduct $10,000, you reduce your taxable income to $340,000. That saves you $3,500 in federal taxes (35% of $10,000), plus whatever your state tax rate is.

Deductions are powerful, but they're not dollar-for-dollar savings. They're percentage savings based on your tax bracket.

Common deductions for doctors:

- 401(k) contributions (as of 2025 Under 50: $23,500; Age 50–59 (and 64+): $23,500 + $7,500 = $31,000; Age 60–63: $23,500 + $11,250 = $34,750)
- HSA contributions (up to $4,300 for individuals, $8,550 for families in 2025)
- Student loan interest (up to $2,500, though this phases out at higher incomes)
- Mortgage interest
- State and local taxes (SALT), capped at $10,000
- Charitable contributions
- Business expenses (if you have a side business or consulting income)

The key insight: Most W-2 doctors are leaving deductions on the table because they don't have a structure to capture them. We'll fix that in the coming chapters.

* * *

PILLAR 2: **Credits**

A credit reduces your tax bill dollar-for-dollar.

This is huge. If you owe $80,000 in taxes and you claim a $10,000 credit, you now owe $70,000. It's a direct reduction.

Credits are rarer than deductions, but they're more powerful.

Common credits for doctors:

- Child Tax Credit (up to $2,000 per child, though this phases out at higher incomes)
- Solar Tax Credit (28-40% of the cost of a solar installation)

- Historic Tax Credit (20% federal credit for rehabilitating historic properties, plus state credits in many states)
- Energy-efficient home improvement credits

The key insight: Most doctors don't even know these credits exist. And because they don't know, they don't plan for them. We'll change that.

* * *

PILLAR 3: Depreciation

Depreciation is an accounting method that allows you to deduct the cost of an asset over time-or, in some cases, all at once.

Here's the concept: When you buy a piece of equipment, a vehicle, or a building, the IRS says, "That asset is going to lose value over time. So we'll let you deduct that loss."

For example, if you buy a $50,000 piece of medical equipment, you might be able to depreciate it over 5 years-deducting $10,000 per year. Or, using bonus depreciation rules, you might be able to deduct the entire $50,000 in Year 1.

* * *

WHY THIS MATTERS FOR DOCTORS:

- If you own your practice building, you can depreciate it.
- If you own rental real estate, you can depreciate it (and accelerate the depreciation using cost segregation).
- If you buy a vehicle for your business, you can depreciate it (potentially up to $28,900 in Year 1 under Section 179).

The key insight: Depreciation is a non-cash deduction. You're not spending money-you're just recognizing the loss of value over time. But it reduces your taxable income just like a cash expense would.

* * *

CLINICAL SCAN: **A Quick Case Example**
Let's see how these three pillars work together.

Dr. Sarah Chen is an employed anesthesiologist earning $400,000 a year. She's married, filing jointly, and has two kids.

Before planning:

- Gross income: $400,000
- Standard deduction: $29,200
- Taxable income: $370,800
- Federal tax: ~$85,000
- State tax (California): ~$35,000
- **Total tax: $120,000**
- **Effective tax rate: 30%**

After planning:
Deductions:

- Maxes out 401(k): $23,500
- Maxes out HSA: $8,550
- Starts a side LLC for expert witness work, deducts $15,000 in home office, travel, and professional expenses
- **Total new deductions: $47,050**

Credits:

- Utilizes Energy Asset Tax Mitigation Strategy and owns solar assets ($60,000 system), claims 30% federal credit: $18,000 (there is additional depreciation benefit, but for simplicity sake we won't go into that here).
- **Total credits: $18,000**

Depreciation:

- Buys a rental property, does cost segregation study, accelerates $50,000 in depreciation in Year 1
- **Total depreciation: $50,000**

After planning:

- Gross income: $400,000
- Total deductions: $29,200 (standard) + $47,050 (new) + $50,000 (depreciation) = $126,250
- Taxable income: $274,500
- Federal tax: ~$55,000
- State tax: ~$22,000
- **Total tax before credits: $77,000**
- **Minus solar credit: $18,000**
- **Total tax after credits: $59,000**
- **Effective tax rate: 14.75%**

Tax savings: $61,000 in Year 1.
That's the power of using all three pillars together.

* * *

THE FRAMEWORK for Evaluating Strategies

Now that you understand the three pillars, here's how to evaluate any tax strategy you encounter:

1. **Which pillar does it fall into?** (Deduction, credit, or depreciation?)
2. **How much will it save me?** (Run the math based on your tax bracket.)
3. **What's the cost to implement?** (Some strategies require upfront investment or ongoing fees.)
4. **What's the risk?** (Is this IRS-approved? Is it likely to be audited?)

5. **Does it align with my goals?** (Just because a strategy saves taxes doesn't mean it's right for you.)

Use this framework every time someone pitches you a "tax strategy." If they can't clearly explain which pillar it falls into and how much it will save you, walk away.

* * *

QUESTIONS TO THINK About

1. **Which of the three pillars am I currently using?** (*Most W-2 doctors are only using basic deductions. Are you using credits? Depreciation?*)
2. **What's one strategy I could implement this year in each pillar?** (*Think: one new deduction, one credit, one depreciation opportunity.*)
3. **Am I evaluating tax strategies with a clear framework, or am I just reacting to what people tell me?** (*Be honest. Do you have a system for evaluating opportunities?*)

* * *

QUESTIONS TO ASK Your CPA

1. **Can you walk me through the three pillars of tax planning and show me where I'm currently optimized and where I'm leaving money on the table?** (*A good CPA should be able to do this easily. If they look confused, that's a red flag.*)
2. **What's one deduction, one credit, and one depreciation strategy we could explore this year?** (*This forces them to think proactively across all three pillars.*)
3. **How do you stay up-to-date on new tax laws and strategies?** (*Tax laws change constantly. Your CPA should be*

attending continuing education courses, reading tax journals, and staying current.)

* * *

The Bottom Line

The three pillars-deductions, credits, and depreciation-are your foundation for tax planning.

Master them, and you'll have a framework for evaluating every strategy you encounter.

Ignore them, and you'll keep overpaying.

Now let's dive into specific strategies you can implement starting today. Please note that the next sections and chapters are provided to show you the art of the possible via examples of some strategies, but it is absolutely not exhaustive.

CHAPTER 4

STRATEGIC DEDUCTIONS

"In this world nothing can be said to be certain, except death and taxes." — *Benjamin Franklin*

"A dollar untracked is a dollar untaxed by you-but taxed by someone else." — *Paavan Kotini*

STRATEGIC DEDUCTIONS

*L*et's talk about deductions-the first pillar of tax planning.

Most doctors think they're already maximizing their deductions. After all, they're contributing to their 401(k), they're deducting their mortgage interest, and they're maybe even deducting student loan interest (if they're under the income phase-out).

But here's the truth: **most W-2 doctors are leaving tens of thousands of dollars in deductions on the table every year.**

Why? Because they don't have a structure to capture them.

Let me explain.

Deductions 101

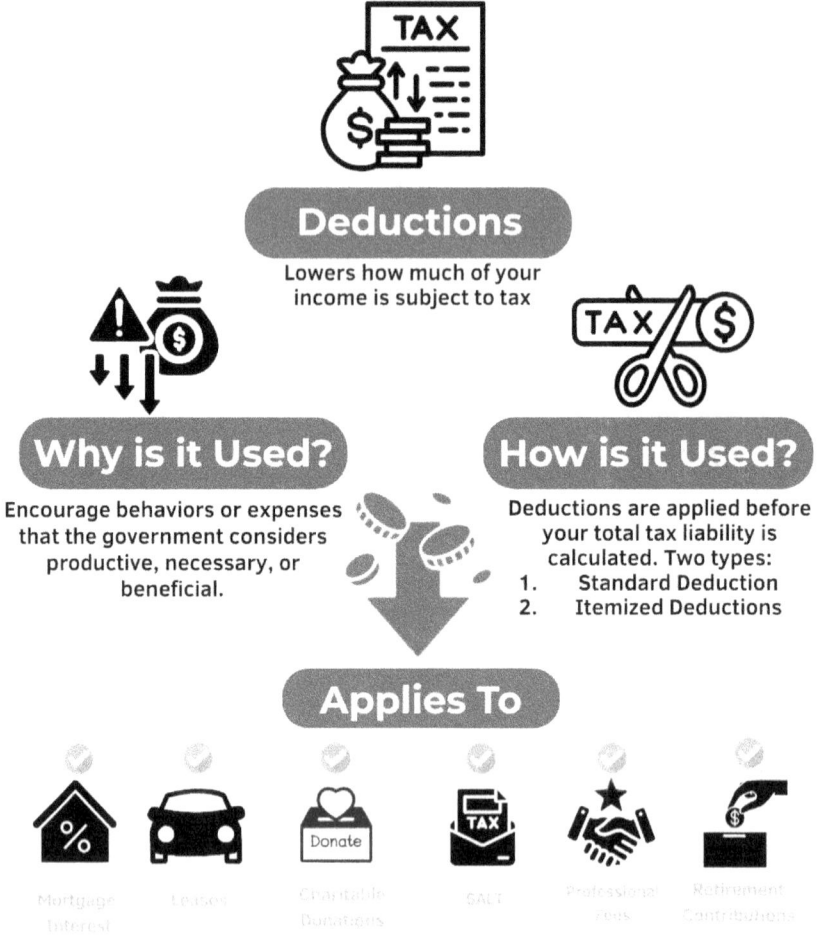

Deductions

Lowers how much of your income is subject to tax

Why is it Used?

Encourage behaviors or expenses that the government considers productive, necessary, or beneficial.

How is it Used?

Deductions are applied before your total tax liability is calculated. Two types:
1.   Standard Deduction
2.   Itemized Deductions

Applies To

Mortgage Interest   Leases   Charitable Donations   SALT   Professional Fees   Retirement Contributions

Figure 4.1: Deductions reduce taxable income. They are applied before your total tax is calculated, deductions come in two types: **Standard Deductions** (a fixed amount—most common) and **Itemized Deductions** (specific qualified expenses—most people miss on maximizing). Common examples include **mortgage interest, leases, charitable donations, state and local taxes (SALT), professional fees, and retirement contributions** —each helping you keep more of what you earn.

* * *

THE W-2 DOCTOR'S Deduction Problem

When you're a W-2 employee, your deduction opportunities are limited. You can't deduct unreimbursed employee expenses anymore (that went away with the Tax Cuts and Jobs Act of 2017). You can't deduct your commute. You can't deduct your work clothes (unless they're uniforms that can't be worn outside of work).

So what can you deduct?

- Retirement contributions (401(k), HSA)
- Mortgage interest (up to $750,000 in mortgage debt)
- State and local taxes (SALT), capped at $10,000
- Charitable contributions
- Student loan interest (up to $2,500, with income phase-outs)

That's about it.

But here's the key: **if you create a side business structure, you unlock an entirely new category of deductions.**

And I'm not talking about anything shady. I'm talking about legitimate business expenses that you're probably already incurring-you're just not deducting them because you don't have a business entity to run them through.

* * *

THE SIDE BUSINESS Strategy

Let me introduce you to one of the most powerful strategies for W-2 doctors: **the side business LLC.**

Here's how it works:

You form an LLC (Limited Liability Company) for a legitimate side business. This could be:

- Medical consulting
- Expert witness work

- Speaking engagements
- Medical writing or blogging
- Telemedicine
- Medical device consulting
- Teaching or CME instruction

The key is that it has to be a real business with a profit motive. You can't just form an LLC and call it a business-you actually have to do work and generate income (even if it's modest at first).

Once you have a legitimate business, you can deduct business expenses. And suddenly, expenses that weren't deductible as a W-2 employee become deductible as business expenses.

* * *

WHAT CAN YOU DEDUCT?

Here's a non-exhaustive list of business expenses you can deduct if you have a side LLC: ***Disclaimer:*** *Tax rules and deduction limits aren't static. The IRS issues annual inflation adjustments that include updates and changes to more than 60 tax provisions, and estate and trust laws can vary by state —the IRS advises seeking state-specific or professional guidance. Business resources like the U.S. Chamber of Commerce also remind readers that before making any business decision you should consult a professional. Always confirm eligible deductions with a qualified CPA or tax adviser who understands both federal and state regulations.*

1. Home Office

If you use a portion of your home exclusively for business, you can deduct home office expenses. This includes:

- A percentage of your mortgage interest or rent
- A percentage of your utilities
- A percentage of your home insurance
- A percentage of your property taxes (beyond the $10,000 SALT cap)

The IRS allows you to use the simplified method ($5 per square foot, up to 300 square feet, for a max deduction of $1,500) or the actual expense method (which can be much higher if you have a large home office).

Example: Dr. Patel has a 200-square-foot home office in his 2,500-square-foot home. That's 8% of his home. If his annual mortgage interest is $20,000, utilities are $5,000, insurance is $2,000, and property taxes are $15,000, he can deduct 8% of those expenses-$3,360-as a business expense.

2. Travel

If you travel for business-to conferences, speaking engagements, consulting meetings-you can deduct:

- Airfare
- Hotels
- Meals (50% deductible)
- Ground transportation (Uber, rental cars, etc.)
- Conference registration fees

Example: Dr. Kim attends three medical conferences a year. She speaks at two of them (making her attendance business-related) and networks at the third. Total travel expenses: $12,000. All deductible.

3. Continuing Medical Education (CME)/ Continuing Dental Education (CDE)/ Continuing Education (CE)

CE expenses are deductible if they're related to your business. This includes:

- Course fees
- Books and subscriptions
- Online learning platforms
- Travel to CE events (see above)

Example: Dr. Rodriguez spends $5,000 a year on CME courses, medical journals, and UpToDate subscriptions. All deductible.

4. Professional Dues and Licensing

- Medical license renewal fees
- DEA registration
- Professional association memberships (AMA, specialty societies, etc.)
- Malpractice insurance (if you pay it yourself)

Example: Dr. Thompson pays $3,000 a year in licensing fees, $2,000 in association dues, and $8,000 in malpractice insurance. Total: $13,000. All deductible.

5. Technology and Equipment

- Computers and tablets
- Software subscriptions
- Medical/dental equipment (if you use it for your side business)
- Cell phone (percentage used for business)

Example: Dr. Nguyen buys a new MacBook Pro for $3,000 and an iPad for $1,000. She uses them 70% for her consulting business. She can deduct $2,800 in Year 1 (using bonus depreciation).

6. Marketing and Advertising

- Website hosting and design
- Business cards
- Social media advertising
- SEO and content marketing

Example: Dr. Garcia builds a website for her telemedicine practice. Cost: $5,000. She also spends $2,000 on Google Ads. Total: $7,000. All deductible.

7. Meals

- Business meals (50% deductible)
- Client entertainment (50% deductible, with limitations)

Example: Dr. Lee takes a potential consulting client to dinner. Bill: $200. Deduction: $100.

8. Retirement Contributions (Beyond Your W-2 401(k))

If your side business generates income, you can set up a Solo 401(k) or SEP IRA and contribute additional pre-tax dollars.

Example: Dr. Patel's consulting business generates $50,000 in net income. He contributes $12,500 (25% of net income) to a SEP IRA. That's an additional $12,500 deduction on top of his W-2 401(k) contribution.

* * *

CLINICAL SCAN: **The Math**

Let's run a real example.

Dr. Emily Carter is an employed cardiologist earning $450,000 a year. She's in the 35% federal tax bracket and pays 9.3% California state tax (44.3% combined marginal rate).

She starts a side LLC for medical consulting and expert witness work. In Year 1, she generates $30,000 in consulting income.

Here are her deductible business expenses:

- Home office: $4,000
- Travel to conferences: $8,000
- CME and subscriptions: $3,000
- Professional dues and licensing: $5,000
- Technology (laptop, iPad): $3,000
- Marketing (website, business cards): $2,000
- Meals: $1,000
- **Total deductions: $26,000**

Her net business income: $30,000 −$26,000 = $4,000.

But here's the key: **those $26,000 in deductions reduce her taxable income.**

Tax savings: $26,000 × 44.3% = **$11,518.**

She paid $11,518 less in taxes because she structured her side income as a business and captured deductions she was already incurring.

And that's just Year 1. Over 30 years, that's $345,540 in tax savings (not accounting for inflation or income growth).

* * *

THE ACCOUNTABLE PLAN: A Secret Weapon

Here's an advanced strategy that most doctors don't know about: **the accountable plan.**

An accountable plan is an IRS-approved reimbursement arrangement that allows your business to reimburse you for business expenses-tax-free.

Here's how it works:

1. You incur a business expense (e.g., travel to a conference).
2. You submit a reimbursement request to your business (with receipts and documentation).
3. Your business reimburses you.
4. The reimbursement is not taxable income to you, and it's a deductible expense for your business.

This is especially powerful if you have a spouse or family member on your payroll. You can reimburse them for business expenses, and those reimbursements are tax-free to them and deductible to your business.

Example: Dr. Patel's wife helps with administrative tasks for his consulting business. He pays her $20,000 a year. She travels to a conference with him (legitimately helping with business tasks). The business reimburses her $5,000 for travel expenses. That $5,000 is tax-free to her and deductible to the business.

* * *

COMMON MISTAKES TO **Avoid**

Before we move on, let's talk about common mistakes doctors make with deductions:

Mistake #1: Not tracking expenses.

If you don't track it, you can't deduct it. Use an app like Quick-Books Self-Employed, Expensify, or even a simple spreadsheet. Track everything.

Mistake #2: Mixing personal and business expenses.

Keep separate bank accounts and credit cards for your business. The IRS hates commingling.

Mistake #3: Deducting personal expenses as business expenses.

This is fraud. Don't do it. Only deduct legitimate business expenses.

Mistake #4: Not documenting expenses.

Keep receipts. Keep mileage logs. Keep records of business meals (who you met with, what you discussed). If you get audited, documentation is everything.

* * *

QUESTIONS TO THINK **About**

1. **How many professional expenses am I currently tracking?** *(If the answer is "none" or "I don't know," that's a problem.)*
2. **Could any "personal" expenses have a legitimate business tie-in?** *(Think: travel, technology, home office, meals.)*
3. **Do I have a side business structure, or am I leaving deductions on the table?** *(If you're doing any consulting, speaking, or side work, you should have an LLC.)*

* * *

QUESTIONS TO ASK YOUR CPA

1. **What expenses am I missing that could qualify as deductions?** *(A good CPA should be able to review your situation and identify opportunities.)*
2. **Do you recommend an accountable plan for tracking expenses?** *(If they don't know what an accountable plan is, that's a red flag.)*
3. **Should I form an LLC for my side income, and if so, how should it be taxed?** *(There are different ways to structure an LLC: sole proprietorship, S-corp, partnership. Your CPA should help you choose the right structure.)*

* * *

THE BOTTOM LINE

Deductions are the foundation of tax planning. But most W-2 doctors aren't maximizing them because they don't have a structure to capture them.

The solution? **Create a side business structure and start tracking your expenses.**

You're probably already incurring these expenses. You're just not deducting them.

Let's change that.

* * *

ADDITIONAL INSIGHTS & Action Steps

Your ability to claim deductions is limited only by your willingness to document, categorize and plan ahead. Think of deductions as strategic investments in your future rather than mere tax tricks. When you create or join a side business, you open a world of deductible expenses that would otherwise be paid with after-tax dollars. Travel to medical conferences? It can be an educational expense. That home office where you chart and plan? It may be partially deductible when you run a legitimate side enterprise. Even the professional development courses you take to sharpen your skills can reduce your taxable income if they relate to your business.

Consider **Dr. Emily**, a dermatologist who moonlights as a telemedicine consultant. She formed a small S-corporation to house her consulting income. By establishing an accountable plan, she reimburses herself for a portion of her home internet, mobile phone and dedicated office space. She also deducts equipment purchases, continuing education and marketing costs. The result: her side hustle not only generates additional revenue but also creates thousands of dollars in deductions that offset her clinical income. Her mindset shifted from, "I hope I can write this off," to, "How can I structure my life so that my spending supports both my mission and my bottom line?"

To implement your own strategic deductions, follow these action steps:

- **Identify a business activity you enjoy.** Whether it's telehealth, speaking, expert witness work or developing a medical device, pick something that aligns with your interests and offers real value.
- **Formalize the entity.** Work with a qualified professional to determine whether an LLC, S-corp or partnership makes sense. Register it properly and obtain an EIN.
- **Create an accountable plan.** Document the business use of your home, vehicle, technology and other mixed-use assets. Reimburse yourself from your business for legitimate expenses and keep copies of receipts.
- **Track every expenditure.** Use accounting software or hire a bookkeeper to categorize expenses as you go. The IRS loves contemporaneous records.
- **Coordinate with your personal taxes.** Make sure deductions flow through correctly, especially if you have multiple income streams. A seasoned tax advisor can help you align the moving parts.

When you treat deductions as part of your overall strategy instead of an afterthought, you'll notice more dollars staying in your pocket and less slipping away unnoticed. Strategic deductions aren't about stretching the rules; they're about learning the rules and playing the game with intention.

CHAPTER 5

THE GOLDEN PRESCRIPTION

"Giving is not just about making a donation; it's about making a difference."
—Kathy Calvin

"Tax credits aren't gifts; they're the government's way of saying, 'You invested in what matters.'" —Paavan Kotini

THE GOLDEN PRESCRIPTION

$\mathscr{L}$et's talk about tax credits—the second pillar of tax planning.

If deductions are good, credits are great. Why? Because **credits reduce your tax bill dollar-for-dollar.**

Remember: a deduction reduces your taxable income, which saves you money based on your tax bracket. But a credit reduces your actual tax bill.

If you owe $100,000 in taxes and you claim a $20,000 credit, you now owe $80,000. It's a direct, immediate reduction.

The problem? Most doctors don't know these credits exist. And because they don't know, they don't plan for them.

Let's fix that.

Tax Credits 101

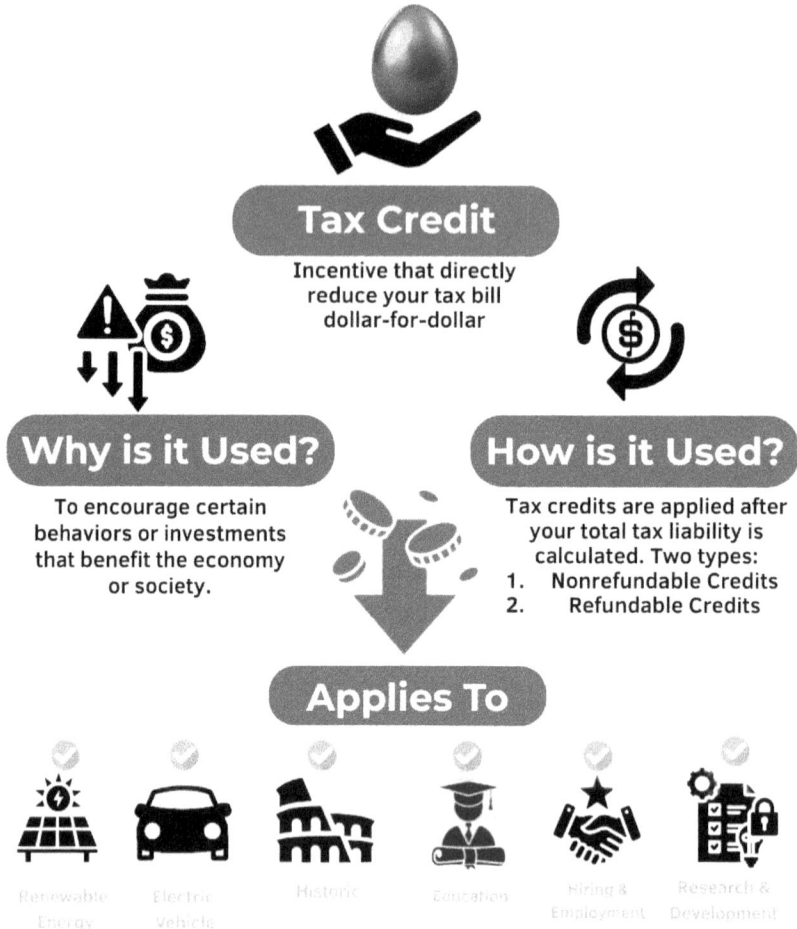

Tax Credit

Incentive that directly
reduce your tax bill
dollar-for-dollar

Why is it Used?

To encourage certain
behaviors or investments
that benefit the economy
or society.

How is it Used?

Tax credits are applied after
your total tax liability is
calculated. Two types:
1. Nonrefundable Credits
2. Refundable Credits

Applies To

| Renewable Energy | Electric Vehicle | Historic | Education | Hiring & Employment | Research & Development |

Figure 5.1: Tax credits reward you for doing good for your business, your community, and the economy. From renewable energy to R&D, education, and job creation, credits reduce your tax bill dollar-for-dollar.There are two kinds: 1) Nonrefundable Credits can reduce your tax bill to zero, but not below it. 2) Refundable Credits can give you a refund even if you owe no tax.

* * *

THE ENERGY ASSET Tax Mitigation Strategy Credit Strategy: Dr. Chen's $340,000 Tax Refund

Dr. Lisa Chen stared at her tax projection in disbelief. March 2025, and her CPA had just delivered the news: she owed $410,000 in federal taxes.

"How is that even possible?" she asked. "I paid quarterly estimates all year."

Her CPA pointed to the numbers. "Your practice had an exceptional year. The surgery center sale closed in December. The hospital bonus you weren't expecting. Your income hit $1.8 million. Federal tax: $410,000."

Lisa felt the familiar knot in her stomach-the one every high-earning physician knows. You work 60-hour weeks, you build wealth, and then you write a check to the IRS for more than most Americans earn in a decade.

"Can we do anything?"

Her CPA shrugged. "Not much at this point. Most strategies need to be in place before year-end. You could make a big charitable donation, but that only saves 37 cents per dollar. To save $150,000 in taxes, you'd have to give away $400,000."

Lisa drove home in frustrated silence. That evening, she called her quarterback at Kotini & Kotini.

"Tell me there's something we can do," she said.

"Actually," he replied, "there is. It's called the Energy Asset Tax Mitigation Strategy. And it might be exactly what you need."

The Strategy Explained

The federal government offers a 30% Investment Tax Credit (ITC) for renewable energy investments. When you invest in projects such as solar energy, you can immediately claim 30% of your investment as a tax credit, plus additional depreciation benefits.

Dr. Chen's Numbers:

- Tax liability: $410,000
- Investment needed: $410,000 ÷ 30% = $1,366,667
- Rounded to: **$1,400,000**

What She Got:
Immediate (2025):

- Investment tax credit (30%): $420,000
- Bonus depreciation deduction: $280,000
- Tax savings from depreciation: $103,600 (at 37% rate)
- **2025 federal tax after credits: $0**
- Excess credits available for carryback: $10,000

Carryback to 2022:

- Credits applied: $10,000
- **Refund from IRS: $10,000**

Ongoing (2026-2030):

- Remaining depreciation over 5 years: $420,000
- Tax savings: $155,400
- **Total depreciation benefit: $259,000**

Equipment Sale (2030):

- Estimated proceeds at 65% recovery: $910,000
- Tax on gain: ~$80,000
- **Net proceeds: $830,000**

Total Strategy Results:

- Cash invested: $1,400,000
- Tax benefits: $679,000
- Equipment sale: $830,000
- **Total return: $1,509,000**
- **Net gain: $109,000 over 6 years**

"So I basically break even on the investment itself," Lisa said, "but I save $410,000 in taxes I would have paid anyway."

"Exactly. And that $410,000 you didn't pay? You can invest it. At 8% annual return over six years, that's worth $648,000."

The Catches:

1. **The 100-Hour Rule:** You must demonstrate "material participation" by logging at least 100 hours per year of business activity related to solar investment. Remember this is a real business with economic sustenance, it just has great tax benefits that can offset other income.
2. **Liquidity:** Its tied up in the solar assets you purchase. You do get the tax benefit that typically will exceed the contributions.
3. **Equipment Value Risk:** Depending on the strategy and the operator risk could be there or mitigated.
4. **Audit Risk:** Material participation documentation is critical.

Lisa's Decision:

She invested $1,400,000 in November 2025. By April 2026, her $410,000 tax bill was eliminated, and she received a $10,000 refund from 2022.

* * *

The Historic Tax Credit (20% Federal + State Stack)

This one's a bit more niche, but if you're in the right situation, it's incredibly powerful.

The Historic Tax Credit (HTC) is a federal tax credit for rehabilitating historic buildings. If you buy and renovate a building that's listed on the National Register of Historic Places (or located in a registered historic district), you can claim a **20% federal tax credit** on your qualified rehabilitation expenses.

But here's where it gets interesting: **many states offer additional state historic tax credits that stack on top of the federal credit.**

For example:

- Missouri: 25% state credit
- Ohio: 25% state credit
- Pennsylvania: 25% state credit
- Virginia: 25% state credit
- Massachusetts: 20% state credit

So you could potentially get a **45% total tax credit** (20% federal + 25% state) on your renovation costs.

Example: You buy a historic building for $500,000 and spend $500,000 renovating it (total investment: $1 million). You claim:

- 20% federal credit on $500,000 = $100,000
- 25% state credit on $500,000 = $125,000
- **Total credits: $225,000**

Your net investment: $1,000,000 —$225,000 = $775,000.
And now you own a $1 million building for $775,000.

Who should consider this?

This strategy works best for doctors who:

- Live in a state with a strong state historic tax credit
- Are interested in real estate investing
- Have a high tax liability ($100,000+ per year)
- Are willing to deal with the complexity of a historic renovation

Key details:

- The building must be income-producing (commercial or rental residential)

- The renovation must be "substantial"-generally, you need to spend at least as much on renovation as the building's purchase price
- You have to follow historic preservation guidelines
- The credit is claimed over 5 years (you get 20% of the credit each year for 5 years)

* * *

LEVERAGED Charitable Donation ($1 → $5 Deduction)

Okay, this one's technically a deduction, not a credit-but it's so powerful that I'm including it here.

Here's the concept: Leveraged Charitable Donations allow **high-income taxpayers to use a charitable entity**-such as a donor-advised fund or charitable LLC-to make large, tax-deductible contributions while retaining some strategic control over the funds. By donating appreciated assets or using structured financing, clients can **significantly reduce their current taxable income**, avoid **capital gains taxes**, and **support causes they care about.** This approach not only maximizes **tax efficiency** but also enhances **philanthropic impact. 3-5x in contribution amount. Can carry forward any deductions up to 5 years.**

You can donate appreciated assets (like stock or real estate) to a donor-advised fund (DAF) and deduct the fair market value-without paying capital gains tax.

* * *

CLINICAL SCAN: The Genetics of Giving —A Leveraged Charitable Donation in Action

Patient: Dr. Kimberly S., 45, Endocrinologist, California
Condition: High-income fatigue with acute tax exposure
Prescription: The *Genetics Leveraged Charitable Donation Strategy*
Background

Dr. Kimberly's practice thrived in 2024, generating **$900,000 of**

taxable income. Despite maxing out her retirement plans and 199A deductions, she was still staring at a **combined federal and state tax bill north of 45 %**. Her goals?

- Support medical research and community health causes she's passionate about
- Create immediate tax relief
- Retain flexibility in directing future grants

Treatment Plan

Her advisor prescribed a **Leveraged Charitable Donation (LCD)** strategy utilizing a **Genetics-based Charitable Partnership**-a structured program with a **5:1 valuation ratio** (wholesale access price → appraised value).

- **Contribution (cash outlay):** $50,000
- **Appraised charitable value:** $250,000
- **Vehicle used:** Donor-Advised Fund (DAF) under a charitable LLC umbrella
- **AGI limit applied:** 50 % of AGI for the charitable deduction
- **Carry-forward:** Any unused deduction can roll forward for 5 years

Outcome

By contributing $50,000 of capital to the partnership, Dr. Kimberly received an appraised charitable contribution of **$250,000**.

With her AGI at $900,000, she could immediately deduct **up to $450,000 (50 % limit)** in charitable contributions-including this new $250,000 gift.

TAX SAVINGS CALCULATION:
Charitable deduction used (2024): $250,000
Marginal tax rate (Fed + CA ≈ 45 %): 45 %
Estimated tax savings: **$112,500**

. . .

NET EFFECT: Dr. Kimberly invested $50,000, received a $250,000 deduction, and reduced her current-year taxes by **$112,500**-while endowing future grants to medical causes through her DAF.

She retained advisory privileges to recommend how and when the charitable funds are deployed, giving her both **control and impact**.

* * *

BOTTOM LINE

- **Leverage ratio:** 3–5× typical contribution amount
- **Deduction limits:** 30–60 % of AGI (depending on structure and asset type)
- **Carry-forward:** Up to 5 years for unused deductions
- **Ideal for:** High-income earners, business owners, and charitably inclined professionals with appreciated assets or liquidity events

But here's where it gets interesting: What if you want to make a donation of a property or other asset. **You can donate assets that have appreciated significantly, giving you a much larger deduction than the cash you originally invested. Leveraged because it has appreciated over time.**

Example: Ten years ago, you bought $50,000 worth of Apple stock. Today, it's worth $250,000. If you sold it, you'd pay 20% federal capital gains tax ($40,000) plus 3.8% net investment income tax ($7,600)-a total of $47,600 in taxes.

Instead, you donate the stock to a donor-advised fund.

You get a $250,000 charitable deduction (saving you $110,000 in taxes if you're in the 44% combined federal/state bracket), and you avoid the $47,600 in capital gains tax.

Total tax savings: $157,600.

And you still control when and where the money goes (through the donor-advised fund).

This is what I call a **leveraged charitable donation**: you turn $50,000 in original investment into $250,000 in tax deductions-a 5x leverage. Leveraged charitable giving isn't about gaming the system-it's about aligning generosity with strategy. When structured properly, it allows physicians to redirect what would have gone to taxes into causes that heal the world.

* * *

CLINICAL SCAN: **Leveraged Charitable Donation in Action**

Dr. Jennifer Wu is a dermatologist in California earning $550,000 a year. She pays about $200,000 in federal and state taxes.

She bought $100,000 worth of Tesla stock five years ago. Today, it's worth $500,000.

She wants to donate to charity, but she also wants to maximize her tax benefit.

Option 1: Sell the stock, pay capital gains tax, donate the cash.

- Capital gains tax: $80,000 (20% federal + 13.3% California)
- Cash available to donate: $420,000
- Charitable deduction: $420,000
- Tax savings from deduction: $185,000 (44% combined rate)
- **Net tax benefit: $105,000**

Option 2: Donate the stock directly to a donor-advised fund.

- Capital gains tax: $0
- Charitable deduction: $500,000
- Tax savings from deduction: $220,000 (44% combined rate)
- **Net tax benefit: $220,000**

By donating the stock instead of selling it, she saves an additional $115,000 in taxes.

* * *

R&D Tax Credits for Practice Owners
The Hidden Gold Mine You're Probably Overlooking

When most physicians or dentists hear *"Research & Development,"* they think of pharmaceutical companies, biotech firms, or major device manufacturers. But under IRS rules, the definition of qualified R&D is much broader—and medical and dental practices often qualify without realizing it.

The R&D Tax Credit is designed to reward innovation in processes, technology, and patient care. If you've improved how you deliver medicine, manage data, or operate your practice, there's a good chance you qualify.

WHAT QUALIFIES AS R&D in a Medical or Dental Practice

If your team has done any of the following, you may be eligible for substantial credits:

- Developing or testing new treatment protocols — improving patient outcomes or safety.
- Modifying surgical tools or devices — even small innovations count.
- Creating or customizing software — such as EMR systems, patient portals, or scheduling algorithms.
- Improving clinical or administrative processes — reducing wait times, integrating new technologies, or enhancing sterilization.
- Conducting internal studies or pilot programs — such as new procedures or recovery protocols.
- Quality improvement initiatives — measuring and refining efficiency or outcomes.

The Numbers

- Federal Credit: typically 6%–10% of qualified research expenses.
- State Credits: available in over 30 states, ranging from 5%–20% (varies by state).
- Typical Savings: $50,000–$250,000 per year for qualifying practices.
- Lookback Period: claim credits for up to three prior open tax years.

* * *

CLINICAL SCAN: **R&D Credits in Action**
Dr. Patel's Orthopedic Practice
Revenue: $3 million | Staff: 8
Over the past year, Dr. Patel's team:

- Developed a new post-surgical recovery protocol
- Modified surgical tools for precision
- Built a custom patient-monitoring app
- Implemented a new sterilization workflow

Qualified R&D Expenses: $600,000
Federal Credit (8%): $48,000
State Credit (CA – 15%): $90,000
Total Tax Savings: **$138,000**
Cost of R&D Study: ($15,000–$25,000)
Net Benefit: **$113,000–$123,000**
Dr. Patel didn't know these activities qualified until his proactive CPA identified them in a planning session.

* * *

POST-OBBBA UPDATE: **R&D Gets Its Spark Back**
Before the One Big Beautiful Bill Act (OBBBA), businesses were required to capitalize and amortize R&D expenses over five years, a

burdensome rule that deterred many smaller practices from pursuing the credit.

OBBBA reversed that requirement, restoring the ability to fully expense R&D costs in the year incurred—a game-changer for medical and dental professionals.

This change makes the R&D credit not just more lucrative but more immediate. You can now claim both the deduction and the credit in the same tax year, supercharging your after-tax ROI on innovation.

ACTION STEPS

1. Review Your Last Three Years (2022–2024).
2. The statute of limitations is closing soon. File now to capture credits before they expire.
3. File a Form 3115 if Needed.
4. If your practice capitalized prior R&D expenses, you can elect a Change in Accounting Method via Form 3115— avoiding the need to amend returns.
5. Get a Professional R&D Study.
6. Work with a specialist familiar with both IRS audit standards and medical/dental operations to document qualified projects.
7. Know the Rule of Thumb (for Dentists).
8. If your practice mills 800+ crowns in-house annually, a formal R&D study is almost always worthwhile.

* * *

SIDEBAR: **The R&D Revival (Post-OBBBA)**

Prior to OBBBA (Pre-2025):

R&D costs had to be capitalized and amortized over five years, delaying the deduction.

Now (Post-2025):

Practices can fully deduct and claim R&D costs in the same year, dramatically improving cash flow.

Why It Matters:

For innovative medical and dental practices, this could translate into six-figure annual tax savings and faster reinvestment into technology, staffing, or facility upgrades.

* * *

Who Should Explore R&D Credits

- Practice owners with multiple employees or departments
- Offices that develop or test new workflows or procedures
- Practices that build, customize, or integrate new software systems
- Dental practices with in-house milling, lab, or manufacturing capabilities
- Medical professionals engaged in continuous improvement or clinical innovation

* * *

R&D Qualification Checklist

Do You Qualify for the R&D Tax Credit?

Step 1: Do You Create or Improve Something?

□ Developed or tested **new treatment protocols**

□ Modified **equipment, tools, or processes**

□ Created or customized **software or EMR systems**

□ Designed **new workflows or efficiency models**

If you checked **any** of these boxes → proceed to Step 2.

Step 2: Was There a Process of Experimentation?

□ You **tested, analyzed, or refined** a process or design

□ The outcome wasn't guaranteed—you tried to **eliminate uncertainty**

□ The work involved **systematic testing**, not just routine updates

If yes → proceed to Step 3.

Step 3: Was It Technological in Nature?

☐ The project relied on **engineering, biological, computer, or physical sciences**

☐ You used data, modeling, or measurement tools to reach a result

If yes → proceed to Step 4.

Step 4: Was It Done in the U.S.?

☐ The activities (or majority of them) occurred **within the United States**

If you answered "yes" to all four steps, your practice likely qualifies for the R&D Tax Credit under IRS Section 41.

* * *

QUICK REFERENCE: **What's New Post-OBBBA**

Rule	Before 2025	Now (Post-OBBBA)
Treatment of R&D Costs	Must be **capitalized and amortized** over 5 years	Can be **fully expensed** in the year incurred
Filing Window	3 prior years (2022–2024)	Still available, but statutes closing soon
Adjustment Option	Amend returns	File **Form 3115** for accounting change
Typical Savings	$50K–$250K/year	Often higher due to full expensing

Figure 5.2: Quick guide to see the R&D changes from pre OBBBA to post OBBBA.

Rule of Thumb (Dentists):

If you mill 800+ crowns in-house annually, it's almost always worth commissioning a formal R+D study.

* * *

81

BOTTOM LINE:

Innovation isn't just good medicine—it's good tax strategy.

Under the new rules, the **R&D Credit is one of the most valuable (and underused) incentives** in the medical and dental sectors. If you're advancing care or improving efficiency, you're likely creating credits without realizing it.

You don't need to be running a lab to qualify.

If you're improving patient outcomes, systems, or technology— you're doing R&D.

Now, thanks to **OBBBA**, you can **deduct it all upfront and claim credits immediately.**

* * *

OTHER COMMON CREDITS **Worth Knowing About**

There are more advanced credits that your advanced tax planning team should be able to bring to the table, but for now here are a few other credits that might apply to you:

1. Energy-Efficient Home Improvement Credit

If you make energy-efficient improvements to your home (new windows, doors, insulation, HVAC systems), you can claim a credit of up to 30% of the cost, with a maximum credit of $1,200 per year (or $2,000 for heat pumps).

2. Electric Vehicle Credit

If you buy a new electric vehicle, you can claim a credit of up to $7,500 (subject to income limits and vehicle requirements). However, EV credits for both new and used vehicles expire for any vehicle acquired after September 30, 2025.

3. Adoption Credit

If you adopt a child, you can claim a credit of up to $17,280 per child (in 2025) for qualified adoption expenses. beginning in 2026, up to $5,000 of the adoption credit becomes refundable (2024 and 2025 credits remain non-refundable).

* * *

QUESTIONS TO THINK **About**

1. **Do I see tax credits as "too complicated"-or as tools worth exploring?** *(Be honest. Complexity is often just unfamiliarity.)*
2. **What causes matter most to me that could benefit from leveraged giving?** *(If you're going to donate anyway, why not maximize the tax benefit?)*
3. **Am I leaving credits on the table because I don't know they exist?** *(Most doctors are.)*

* * *

QUESTIONS TO ASK **Your CPA**

1. **Have you ever helped a client claim solar or historic tax credits?** *(If they haven't, that doesn't mean they can't-but it does mean you'll need to educate them- or find someone who specializes in these credits.)*
2. **Do you know how a leveraged charitable donation works?** *(If they don't, find a CPA who does. This strategy can possibly save you multiple six figures over your career.)*
3. **What credits am I eligible for that we haven't explored yet?** *(A good CPA should be proactively looking for credit opportunities.)*

* * *

THE BOTTOM LINE

Credits are the most powerful tool in tax planning because they reduce your tax bill dollar-for-dollar.

But most doctors don't use them because they don't know they exist.

Now you know.

So let's start planning.

CHAPTER 6

⚜

THE POWER OF DEPRECIATION

"You must know the difference between an asset and a liability, and buy assets. An asset puts money in my pocket. A liability takes money out of my pocket." —Robert Kiyosaki

"Time wears things down. Depreciation just lets you get paid for it." —Paavan Kotini

THE POWER OF DEPRECIATION

$\mathscr{L}$et's talk about the third pillar of tax planning: **depreciation.**

DEPRECIATION IS one of the most misunderstood-and underutilized-tools in the tax code. But once you understand it, it becomes one of your most powerful weapons for reducing taxes.

Here's the concept in plain English:

When you buy an asset that will be used in business or to produce income (like a building, a piece of equipment, or a vehicle), the IRS says, "That asset is going to lose value over time. So we'll let you deduct that loss."

The key insight: **Depreciation is a non-cash deduction.**

You're not spending money. You're just recognizing the loss of value over time. But it reduces your taxable income just like a cash expense would.

Let me show you how powerful this is.

Depreciation 101

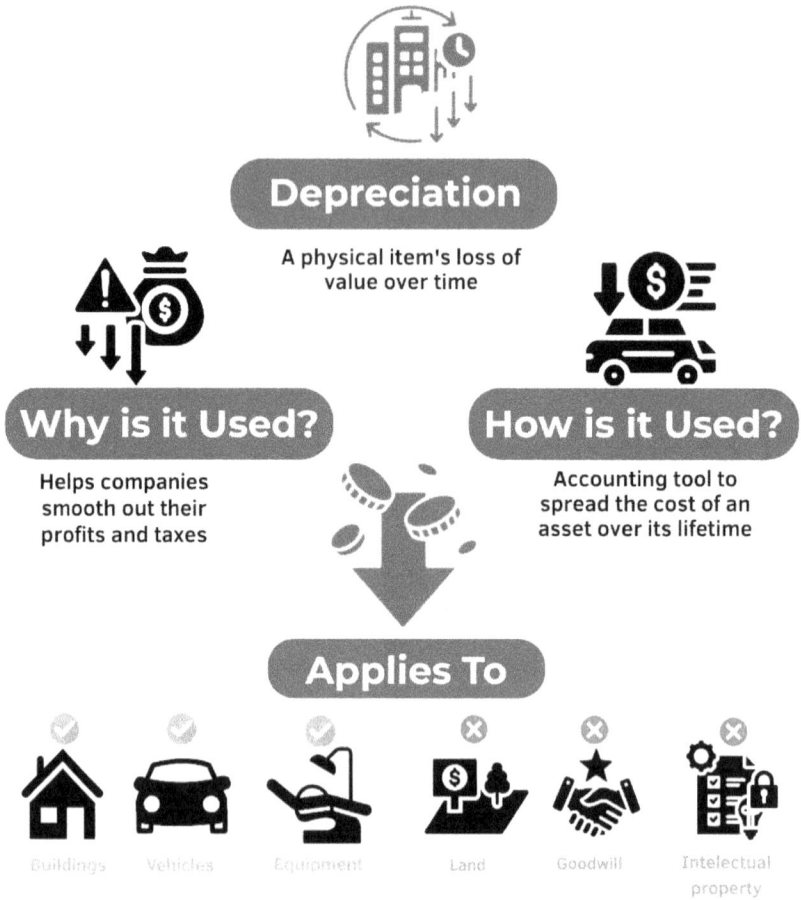

Depreciation

A physical item's loss of value over time

Why is it Used?

Helps companies smooth out their profits and taxes

How is it Used?

Accounting tool to spread the cost of an asset over its lifetime

Applies To

| Buildings | Vehicles | Equipment | Land | Goodwill | Intelectual property |

Figure 6.1: Depreciation allows you to deduct the declining value of assets over time, reducing taxable income without cash outlay. Applies to buildings, vehicles, and equipment. Does not apply to land, goodwill, and intellectual property.

* * *

REAL ESTATE DEPRECIATION

Let's start with real estate, because this is where most doctors can benefit immediately.

When you buy a commerical rental property, the IRS lets you depreciate the building (not the land) over 27.5 years for residential property or 39 years for commercial property.

Example: You buy a rental property for $500,000. The land is worth $100,000, and the building is worth $400,000.

You can depreciate the building over 27.5 years: $400,000 ÷ 27.5 = **$14,545 per year in depreciation.**

That's a $14,545 deduction every year-without spending a dime.

If you're in the 40% combined federal/state tax bracket, that saves you $5,818 in taxes every year.

Over 27.5 years, that's $160,000 in tax savings.

But here's where it gets really interesting: **cost segregation.**

* * *

Cost Segregation: Accelerating Depreciation

Cost segregation is a strategy that allows you to accelerate depreciation by reclassifying parts of a building into shorter depreciation schedules.

Here's how it works:

Normally, you depreciate a building over 27.5 or 39 years. But a building isn't just one asset-it's made up of many components:

- The structure (walls, roof, foundation)
- Electrical systems
- Plumbing
- HVAC
- Flooring
- Landscaping
- Parking lots
- Fixtures

Some of these components can be depreciated over much shorter periods:

- 5 years (carpeting, appliances, landscaping)
- 7 years (furniture, fixtures)
- 15 years (parking lots, sidewalks, fencing)

A cost segregation study is an engineering analysis that breaks down your building into these components and reclassifies them into shorter depreciation schedules.

The result? You can deduct 30-40% of the building's value in Year 1 (using bonus depreciation rules). However, for *residential* rentals, passive loss limitations often prevent taxpayers from benefiting from the large Year-1 deductions. Better suited for commerical properties.

Clinical Scan: Cost Segregation in Action

Dr. Lisa Martinez buys a commercial property for $600,000 ($500,000 building, $100,000 land).

Without cost segregation:

- Annual depreciation: $500,000 ÷ 27.5 = $18,182
- Tax savings (40% bracket): $7,273 per year

With cost segregation:

- A cost segregation study identifies $200,000 in components that can be depreciated over 5, 7, or 15 years.
- Using bonus depreciation, she deducts $200,000 in Year 1.
- Tax savings (40% bracket): **$80,000 in Year 1.**

That's an extra $72,727 in tax savings in Year 1 compared to straight-line depreciation.

Cost of the study: $5,000-$10,000. **Return on investment:** 7x to 14x in Year 1 alone.

* * *

Bonus Depreciation & Section 179: The Equipment Purchase That Pays for Itself

Let's talk about equipment and vehicles-another powerful depreciation opportunity.

Bonus Depreciation lets you deduct most (or all) of the equipment cost in the year you buy it.

The Timeline (post-OBBB):

- Property placed in service after January 19, 2025: **100% bonus depreciation (permanent)**

Section 179 is similar but with two key differences:

1. Cannot create or increase a business loss (income limitation)
2. Maximum deduction: $2,500,000 (2025+, thanks to OBBB)

* * *

Clinical Scan: Dr. Park's $850,000 MRI Machine

Dr. Michael Park needed an MRI machine for his practice-an $850,000 purchase.

With 100% bonus depreciation (2025):

- Purchase price: $850,000
- Immediate deduction: $850,000
- Tax savings (at 40% combined rate): **$340,000**

"I spend $850,000 and immediately save $340,000 in taxes?" Michael asked.

"Correct. Your after-tax cost is really $510,000. Plus you still own the $850,000 asset, and it starts generating revenue immediately."

* * *

VEHICLE RULES: The Heavy SUV Advantage (Post-OBBBA Update)

Vehicle deductions remain one of the most misunderstood—and most powerful—tax opportunities for practice owners. The rules differ depending on the weight of the vehicle, but thanks to the **One Big Beautiful Bill Act (OBBBA)**, the combination of **Section 179 expensing** and **permanent 100% bonus depreciation** has made 2025 one of the most favorable years in history to purchase qualifying vehicles for business use.

* * *

PASSENGER VEHICLES (Under 6,000 lbs GVWR)

- **Maximum first-year depreciation: $20,400 for 2025** (*indexed annually for inflation*).
- Subject to the IRS's **"luxury auto" limits**, which cap how much depreciation can be claimed each year over the vehicle's recovery period.
- **Bonus depreciation:** *Eliminated* for passenger vehicles beginning in **2025**, following the OBBBA alignment with the revised **Section 280F** limitations.
- As a result, first-year write-offs are limited to the **standard MACRS depreciation schedule**, rather than 100% bonus depreciation.
- Subsequent annual limits (Year 2, Year 3, and Year 4+) remain capped and phased in over time.

* * *

HEAVY SUVs, Trucks, and Vehicles (Over 6,000 lbs GVWR)

- Eligible for **Section 179 expensing** up to **$30,500** (2025).
- Any remaining cost basis qualifies for **100% bonus depreciation** under OBBBA (permanent).

- The vehicle must be **used more than 50% for qualified business purposes** to claim accelerated deductions.

* * *

QUICK CONTEXT

The One Big Beautiful Bill Act (OBBBA) permanently reinstated 100% bonus depreciation for qualifying business property but excluded passenger autos under 6,000 lbs GVWR from that rule to close perceived abuse loopholes. This means heavy vehicles (SUVs, trucks, large vans) still qualify for immediate expensing, while passenger sedans and smaller crossovers return to the traditional multi-year depreciation limits.

Example: The Heavy SUV Play

Dr. James Park purchased a **$75,000 SUV (6,800 lbs GVWR)** and uses it **70% for business.**

Business Basis: $75,000 × 70% = $52,500

Section 179 Deduction: $30,500

Remaining Basis Eligible for Bonus Depreciation: $22,000

100% Bonus Depreciation (OBBBA-Permanent): $22,000

Total First-Year Deduction: $52,500

Approximate Tax Savings (at 40% marginal rate): $21,000

Because OBBBA made 100% bonus depreciation permanent, Dr. Park can now fully expense the entire business portion of qualifying heavy-vehicle purchases in the first year—without worrying about phased-down percentages after 2026.

Critical Rule: Document Business Use

The IRS now uses AI-based audit selection, and vehicle deductions are a high-visibility trigger.

You must:

Use the vehicle > 50% for business.

Keep contemporaneous mileage logs. Do not reconstruct them later.

* * *

Who Should Do Cost Segregation?
Cost segregation makes sense if:

- You own rental real estate (residential or commercial). However, note that for residential rentals, passive loss limitations often prevent taxpayers from benefiting from the large Year-1 deductions.
- You own your practice building
- The property cost at least $500,000 (below that, the study cost might not be worth it)
- You have a high tax liability ($50,000+ per year)

* * *

Questions to Think About

1. **What major assets have I purchased in the last 3 years?** *(Real estate? Equipment? Vehicles?)*
2. **Did I depreciate them slowly, or accelerate the deduction?** *(If you didn't accelerate, you left money on the table- but you might be able to catch up using a "catch-up" depreciation adjustment.)*
3. **Am I thinking about depreciation proactively, or am I just letting my CPA handle it?** *(Your CPA should be proactive, but you need to ask the right questions.)*

* * *

Questions to Ask Your CPA

1. **Have we run a cost segregation study on my practice building or rental properties?** (*If the answer is no, ask why. If the property is worth $500,000+, a cost segregation study almost always makes sense.*)
2. **Could my vehicle qualify for bonus depreciation under Section 179?** (*If you use a vehicle for business, you should be depreciating it aggressively.*)
3. **Am I maximizing depreciation on all my business assets?** (*A good CPA should be looking for every opportunity to accelerate depreciation.*)

* * *

THE BOTTOM LINE

Depreciation is a non-cash deduction that can save you tens of thousands-or even hundreds of thousands-of dollars in taxes over your career.

But most doctors don't use it because they don't understand it.

Now you do.

So let's put it to work.

* * *

ADDITIONAL INSIGHTS & Action Steps

Depreciation is often described as a phantom expense because no cash leaves your bank account when you claim it. Yet its impact on your tax return is very real. The tax code offers several flavours of depreciation, and understanding how they differ can save you tens of thousands of dollars. Straight-line depreciation spreads the cost of an asset evenly over its useful life. Section 179 allows you to write off the full purchase price of qualifying equipment or software in the year you place it in service, up to an annual limit. Bonus depreciation lets you deduct a percentage of the cost immediately, and it can apply to used property as well.

Dr. Patel, a dentist, purchased a building for his practice. Instead of depreciating the structure over 39 years, he commissioned a cost segregation study. Engineers combed through the property and reclassified components like carpets, cabinets and lighting into 5-, 7- and 15-year property. This accelerated depreciation resulted in an additional $200,000 deduction in the first year alone. Dr. Patel reinvested the tax savings into new equipment and staff training, amplifying the growth of his business.

To make depreciation work for you, keep these steps in mind:

- **List your capital assets.** Identify buildings, equipment, vehicles and software used in your practice or business.
- **Consult a specialist.** Engage a cost segregation firm if you own real estate. Their fee is often a fraction of the immediate tax benefit.
- **Consider Section 179 vs. bonus depreciation.** Section 179 is subject to annual limits and income thresholds, while bonus depreciation is not. Use the combination that suits your cash flow and future plans.
- **Document in-service dates.** An asset must be placed in service before you can claim depreciation. Keep invoices and usage logs.
- **Plan for recapture.**

*** Important *** When you sell or dispose of a depreciated asset, you may have to pay back a portion of the deduction through depreciation recapture. Factor this into your exit strategy.

Depreciation isn't just for real estate moguls. Every doctor who owns equipment, software or buildings can benefit from understanding how and when to claim it. Done correctly, it becomes one of the most powerful levers in your tax toolbox.

CHAPTER 7

WHEN EVERY DOLLAR WORKS TWICE

"The hardest thing in the world to understand is income taxes." – Albert Einstein

"It's not always about getting the greatest rate of return; today, it's more important to get the most tax-efficient rate of return." – Paavan Kotini

WHEN EVERY DOLLAR WORKS TWICE

∝∝∝

A **Shift From ROI to ROT**

In medicine, success depends on accuracy, not aggression. The same holds true for investing.

For decades, people chased ROI (Return on Investment), as if higher numbers alone meant better outcomes.

But the modern wealth builder knows a deeper truth: the Return on Taxes (ROT) often tells the real story.

Every dollar has a job. The question is whether it's working once or twice. When structured correctly, some investments not only earn income but also reduce taxes, letting your wealth compound faster.

This is where the true magic of tax-efficient investing begins.

* * *

THE DIAGNOSTIC VIEW: **A Clinical Scan of Your Capital**

Think of your portfolio like a patient scan. A good clinician doesn't just treat symptoms like "low returns." They look deeper- examining inflammation points such as tax drag, capital leakage, and inefficient income flow.

A tax-efficient investment strategy acts like targeted therapy. It strengthens strong cells (productive assets) and suppresses harmful growth (unnecessary taxes). The goal is a healthy, self-healing wealth system.

Two of the most potent "treatments" for this are Energy Partnerships and Qualified Opportunity Zones (QOZs). Both convert tax liabilities into active capital-so your dollars keep working, even when you're not.

THE ENERGY OF EFFICIENCY: Oil & Gas Partnerships

Energy investments sit in a rare category where the U.S. government actively rewards private investors.

Why? Because national energy independence depends on private capital helping fuel exploration and production.

When structured as drilling partnerships, these programs can offer:

- Up to 90% first-year deductions via Intangible Drilling Costs (IDCs)
- Quarterly cash distributions tied to well productivity
- Potential depletion and depreciation allowances
- Tax-advantaged income from production revenue

It's one of the few places where your investment can simultaneously earn and deduct.

Example: Turning Tax Burdens into Benefits

Let's say Dr. Mehta, an oral surgeon earning $450,000, invests $150,000 in a 2025 drilling program.

- Approximately $135,000 qualifies as deductible IDCs.
- His taxable income drops from $450,000 to $315,000.
- His federal bracket slides from 35% to 24%.

That move can generate an immediate $47,000+ tax savings while maintaining upside potential from production.

Dr. Mehta didn't just make a return. He reclaimed a portion of his taxes as capital to reinvest.

This is what we call two-pocket efficiency:

- One pocket reduces taxes today.
- The other builds income for tomorrow.

(Note: Energy partnerships are speculative and intended for accredited investors. Always review the Private Placement Memorandum and consult your CPA.)

* * *

OPPORTUNITY ZONES: Turning a Decade into a Lifetime of Tax-Free Growth

The Opportunity Zone program was born out of the 2017 Tax Cuts and Jobs Act to channel private investment into underserved communities. For investors, it remains one of the most powerful sequences of tax advantages ever written into law. The **One Big Beautiful Bill (OBBB)** made Qualified Opportunity Zones a permanent feature of the tax code — a material shift in long-term planning. Looking ahead, post-2026 provisions may unlock additional advantages for sellers and long-term investors seeking to compound wealth while supporting community revitalization.

The Opportunity Zone program emerged from the 2017 Tax Cuts and Jobs Act as a way to channel private investment into underserved communities. For investors, it remains one of the most powerful tax-advantaged structures ever legislated. However, two distinct rule sets now exist — the **Pre-OBBB Opportunity Zone program**, which applies to investments made through **December 31, 2026**, and the **Post-OBBB program**, created under the **One Big Beautiful Bill (OBBB)** for investments made after that date.

Pre-OBBB Opportunity Zone Investments (Through December 31, 2026)

- **Deferral:** Investors can defer paying capital-gains tax by reinvesting eligible gains into a Qualified Opportunity Fund (QOF) within 180 days. The deferred gain must be recognized on the earlier of the date the QOF investment is sold or **December 31, 2026.**

- **Reduction:** The former 10% step-up in basis for a 5-year hold applied only to investments made by the end of 2021 (so the 5-year mark would be reached by the 2026 recognition date). That benefit is no longer available for new investments made today.

- **Exclusion:** If a QOZ investment is held for 10 years or more, investors may elect to increase their basis to fair market value upon sale — making all post-acquisition appreciation tax-free. Under the original law, this benefit applies if the investment is sold by **December 31, 2047.**

These rules still offer a powerful combination of deferral and tax-free growth, but the window closes for new investments at the end of 2026.

* * *

POST-OBBB OPPORTUNITY ZONE Investments (After December 31, 2026)

- **Deferral:** Under the OBBB's "Opportunity Zones 2.0," the program becomes permanent, introducing **rolling five-year deferral periods** instead of a fixed 2026 deadline.

- **Step-Up in Basis:** Investors receive a **10% step-up** after 5 years; those investing in designated **rural funds (QROFs)** qualify for a **30% step-up**.

- **Exclusion:** Appreciation on QOZ investments held 10 years or longer remains tax-free when sold. The new law adds a **30-year cap** on tax-free growth before additional appreciation becomes taxable.

* * *

IN SUMMARY

- **Pre-OBBB Opportunity Zone investments** follow the original TCJA framework, with deferral through 2026 and 10-year tax-free appreciation for qualifying holds.

- **Post-OBBB Opportunity Zone investments** establish a **permanent program** beginning 2027, featuring rolling deferrals, renewed basis step-ups, and enhanced rural incentives.

Example: The 10-Year Clinical Cure

Dr. Chen sells her dental practice for $2 million and realizes a $1 million gain. Instead of writing a $238,000 check to the IRS, she reinvests that gain into a Qualified Opportunity Fund focused on sustainable housing.

- Her $238,000 tax payment is deferred until 2026.
- She earns distributions during the holding period.
- In 2036, her investment doubles to $2 million.
- Her gain on that second million? Tax-free.

The result: A decade-long "financial remission," where growth compounds quietly and cleanly.

* * *

COMBINING BOTH STRATEGIES: The Tax Trifecta

For advanced planners, the intersection of Energy Partnerships and Opportunity Zones can create the ultimate proactive strategy.

When structured properly, this blend allows for:

- Immediate tax deductions through Intangible Drilling Costs
- Deferral of capital gains through Opportunity Zone reinvestment
- Tax-free appreciation after a 10-year hold period

In essence, you're stacking deductions, deferrals, and exemptions —turning what would have been taxable income into a perpetual motion machine for wealth creation.

* * *

FROM AVOIDANCE to Alignment

These are not loopholes. They are policy-aligned incentives. Congress designed them to attract capital where the nation needs it most: energy, housing, and innovation.

Smart investors understand that tax strategy isn't about evasion. It's about elevation by channeling capital into vehicles that reward both your portfolio and the public good.

* * *

QUESTIONS TO THINK About

1. **How many of your current investments actually reduce your taxes while generating income?** (*Most portfolios create income that's taxable; few are intentionally designed to produce income that's tax-efficient.*)

2. **Are your dollars working once—or twice—for you?** (*Every dollar should have a dual purpose: earning returns today while reducing tomorrow's tax bill.*)

3. **If you could reallocate "lost" tax payments into active assets, how much faster could your net worth compound?** (*Redirecting tax liabilities into productive investments turns a sunk cost into compounding capital.*)

4. **What's your personal risk tolerance for illiquid, long-term, tax-advantaged investments?** (*Understanding your comfort with limited liquidity helps align your strategy with both cash-flow needs and patience for tax-deferred growth.*)

* * *

QUESTIONS TO ASK **Your CPA**

1. **Could Intangible Drilling Costs reduce my current-year taxable income?** (*These deductions can offset active income immediately if structured and timed properly.*)

2. **How would a drilling fund deduction affect my AMT exposure or self-employment taxes?** (*Certain deductions may lower regular taxable income but have different effects under the Alternative Minimum Tax or self-employment rules.*)

3. **Do I qualify to invest capital gains into a Qualified Opportunity Fund?** (*Eligibility depends on how and when the gain was realized, and whether it meets the 180-day reinvestment window.*)

4. **What would my tax picture look like if I combined a drilling fund with an Opportunity Zone strategy?** (*Layering multiple tax-advantaged vehicles can accelerate deferrals and long-term appreciation, but coordination is essential.*)

5. **Are there any state-level implications or filing requirements I should prepare for?** (*Some states don't*

conform to federal tax incentives, so additional filings or limitations may apply.)

* * *

THE BOTTOM LINE

The wealthiest families don't just make money —they redirect it.

They understand that compounding works best when taxes are minimized and reinvestment is maximized.

Energy partnerships and Opportunity Zone investments show that the government often pays partial tuition for your wealth journey; if you know how to enroll.

When every dollar works twice, you stop being reactive to the tax code and start engineering it to serve you.

* * *

ADDITIONAL INSIGHTS & Action Steps

1. Perform a "Financial MRI." Scan your portfolio for inefficiencies. Identify assets producing high taxable income but low after-tax yield.

2. Evaluate your Tax-to-Wealth Ratio. How many cents of every dollar earned are being lost to taxes and how can they be recovered through structured investments?

3. Explore Accreditation. Many of these opportunities are limited to accredited investors. Determine your eligibility early.

4. Pair Your Team. Have your financial advisor, CPA, and attorney collaborate to design compliant, synergistic tax-mitigation strategies.

5. Commit to Longevity. These aren't get-rich plays; they're stay-rich systems. Patience is part of the profit.

"Proactive planning is not about escaping taxes. It's about transforming them—from what you owe into what you own." - Paavan Kotini

CHAPTER 8

REAL ESTATE AS A TAX STRATEGY

"The hardest thing in the world to understand is the income tax." – Albert Einstein

"Real estate isn't just about location—it's about leveraging appreciation and depreciation for tax relief." – Paavan Kotini

REAL ESTATE AS A TAX STRATEGY

*R*eal estate is often called one of the best tax shelters in America—and for good reason.

Figure 8.1: Investing in real estate can provide tax deductions, depreciation, and long-term wealth growth.

The tax code is designed to **reward ownership and investment**, not consumption. Real estate sits at the heart of that philosophy. When used strategically, it can:

- Generate passive income
- Provide massive tax deductions (through depreciation)
- Build long-term wealth
- Diversify your portfolio beyond paper assets

Yet most doctors don't invest strategically. They either:

- Avoid it (thinking it's risky or too complex)
- Buy a rental property on impulse (without understanding the tax side)
- Invest passively (through REITs or syndications) without optimizing the tax advantages

In this chapter, we'll reframe real estate as a **strategic tax tool—**
not just an investment.

The Tax Benefits of Real Estate

Let's unpack the key advantages one by one.

1. Depreciation: A Paper Deduction with Real Cash Value

Depreciation allows you to deduct the "wear and tear" of a property over time—even when the property is actually appreciating in value.

- **Residential:** 27.5 years
- **Commercial:** 39 years
- **Bonus Depreciation / Cost Segregation:** Accelerate depreciation by breaking assets like fixtures, flooring, and HVAC into 5-, 7-, or 15-year schedules.

Example: A $1M medical office can generate over $200K in year-one deductions with a cost segregation study.

2. 1031 Exchange: Swap, Don't Sell

A 1031 exchange lets you defer capital gains taxes when you reinvest sale proceeds into another "like-kind" property.

- Identify a replacement within **45 days**.
- Close within **180 days**.
- Continue exchanging properties indefinitely to defer tax.

Ultimately, when you pass away, your heirs inherit at a **step-up in basis**—meaning all prior capital gains vanish.

. . .

3. Qualified Business Income (QBI) Deduction

If your real estate qualifies as a **trade or business**, you may deduct up to **20%** of qualified income under Section 199A. *(This often applies to active rental operations, not passive REIT investments.)*

4. Opportunity Zones (OZ)

Investing capital gains into Qualified Opportunity Funds allows:

- **Deferral** of current capital gains until 2027
- **Reduction** of deferred gain (if held ≥ 5 years)
- **Elimination** of new gain after **10 years**. *(An OZ turns a taxable event into a long-term tax-free compounding opportunity.)*

5. Passive Losses and Active Participation

Rental real estate losses can offset other income depending on your involvement.

- **Active participants:** Deduct up to $25,000 of losses (AGI limits apply).
- **Real Estate Professionals (REPS):** Deduct unlimited losses if >50% of your working time and >750 hours/year are in real estate. *(In other words, your "paper losses" can erase real taxes if you qualify.)*

6. Home Office and Mixed-Use Property Deductions

If part of your home is used exclusively for business, you can deduct:

- A portion of **mortgage interest, utilities, insurance, and taxes**
- **Depreciation** on that section of the home *(Your workspace can literally pay rent to yourself.)*

7. Capital Gains Exclusion on Primary Residence

When selling your primary residence:

- **Single:** Exclude up to $250K of gain
- **Married filing jointly:** Exclude up to $500K
- Must have owned and lived in the home for **2 of the last 5 years**. *(A family's home can double as a tax-free growth engine.)*

8. Energy-Efficient Property Credits

- **Investment Tax Credit (ITC):** Up to **30%** credit for solar or renewable systems.
- **Section 179D:** Deductions for commercial buildings improving efficiency (lighting, HVAC, envelope). *(Good for the planet—and even better for your tax bill.)*

9. Charitable Remainder Trusts (CRTs)

A CRT lets you:

- Donate appreciated real estate (avoiding immediate capital gains)
- Receive **lifetime income**
- Deduct a portion of the property's value

- Pass the remainder to charity **tax-free** (*The win-win of philanthropy meets tax strategy.*)

10. 831(B) Captive Insurance + Real Estate

Own multiple properties or commercial buildings? You can form an **831(b) micro-captive** to self-insure risks such as:

- Tenant default, environmental hazards, or business interruption.
- Premiums are deductible, and reserves grow tax-deferred. (*It's how you insure smarter and profit from your own protection.*)

11. Step-Up in Basis

Upon death, heirs inherit property at **fair market value**, not original cost.

This **erases built-in gains** and resets depreciation schedules—creating a generational wealth-transfer advantage. (*A lifetime of deferred gains disappears overnight.*)

* * *

CLINICAL SCAN: REPS in Action
Dr. David and Lisa Park

Dr. Park is a cardiologist earning $450,000. His wife, Lisa, manages their four rental properties worth $2M.

The properties produce $80,000 in income, $40,000 in cash flow, and show a $60,000 paper loss after depreciation.

Lisa qualifies as a **Real Estate Professional**:

- 1,000 hours per year
- More than 50% of her working time in real estate

Their $60,000 loss offsets Dr. Park's W-2 income.

Tax savings: $24,000 per year, or $480,000 over 20 years.

(The tax code rewards those who treat real estate like a business, not a hobby.)

The 1031 Exchange in Action

Dr. Mark Thompson

Bought a rental for $400K, now worth $1.2M.

Depreciation claimed: $200K.

Capital gain on sale: $800K → potential $240K+ tax bill.

Instead, he executes a 1031 exchange:

- Identifies three replacement properties within 45 days
- Closes on a $1.5M apartment within 180 days
- Defers 100% of the gain

Tax due: $0

He reinvests everything, earns more income, more depreciation, and—when he dies—his heirs inherit with a **step-up in basis** that wipes out all deferred gains.

(A well-planned 1031 can convert temporary deferral into permanent elimination.)

* * *

CLINICAL SCAN: **Short-Term Rental Loophole**

Dr. Nguyen

Emergency physician. Purchases a $400K vacation rental.

Spends 150 hours/year managing it (cleaning, bookings, vendors).

Generates $50K income and $30K paper loss via depreciation.

Because she **materially participates** and average guest stays are under 7 days, the loss is considered **active**, not passive.

She deducts the $30K loss directly against W-2 income.

Tax savings: $12,000/year.

(Short-term rentals can blur the line between leisure and leverage.)

* * *

QUESTIONS TO THINK **About**

1. **Am I avoiding real estate because I don't understand it— or because I truly don't want to manage it?** (*Education fixes fear. Clarity prevents regret.*)
2. **Could my spouse qualify as a Real Estate Professional?** (*Shifting REPS status can unlock six-figure deductions.*)
3. **Am I selling property and paying capital gains tax when I could defer it through a 1031 exchange?** (*You may be donating money to the IRS unnecessarily.*)
4. **Have I explored cost segregation to accelerate depreciation?** (*Front-loading deductions boosts early-year cash flow and tax efficiency.*)
5. **Am I prepared to document material participation for short-term rentals?** (*Proving effort can turn passive losses into active deductions.*)

* * *

QUESTIONS TO ASK **Your CPA**

1. **Do I or my spouse qualify as a Real Estate Professional?** (*They should help you track hours and determine if you meet the requirements.*)
2. **Should I consider a cost segregation study on my rental properties?** (*If your properties are worth $500,000+, the answer is almost always yes.*)
3. **Can you explain how a 1031 exchange works and help me execute one?** (*If they've never done a 1031 exchange, you might need to work with a specialist - a Qualified Intermediary.*)

* * *

The Bottom Line

Real estate is the **doctor's tax laboratory,** where cash flow, appreciation, leverage, and tax law all intersect.

It rewards those who learn its language and punishes those who ignore it.

When used intentionally, it can:

- Create lifetime income
- Eliminate entire tax categories
- Transfer wealth tax-free to the next generation

Real estate isn't just where you live —it's where your money learns to grow up.

But it requires education, planning, and often a spouse or partner to help manage it.

If you're willing to put in the work (or hire the right team), real estate can save you six to seven figures in taxes over your career.

* * *

Additional Insights & Action Steps

Real estate isn't just a place to hang your white coat; it's a potent tax strategy when approached with intention. Owning rental property allows you to deduct expenses, claim depreciation and potentially qualify for the coveted real estate professional status (REPS), which can unlock passive losses against active income. Leveraging a 1031 exchange lets you sell a property and defer capital gains taxes as long as you reinvest the proceeds into another like-kind property within specific timelines. Short-term rentals can combine the best of both worlds-cash flow and depreciation-if you meet the material participation rules.

Take **Dr. Johnson**, an emergency physician who purchased a vacation rental near a ski resort. By materially participating-advertising, managing bookings and coordinating cleanings-he qualified as a real estate professional for that property. The resulting losses from depreciation offset a significant portion of his clinical income. Later, he sold a duplex he had owned for ten years and rolled the gains into a larger apartment building via a 1031 exchange, deferring $300,000 in taxes. The additional cash flow helped him cut back his shifts without sacrificing income.

Here are your marching orders:

- **Educate yourself on REPS criteria.** You must spend more than 750 hours and more than half of your working time on real estate activities to qualify. Documentation is key.
- **Run the numbers.** Evaluate cash flow, taxes and appreciation before buying. A property should make sense even without the tax benefits.
- **Consider cost segregation.** Accelerate depreciation on short-term rentals to supercharge deductions in the early years.
- **Plan for exit using 1031 exchanges.** Identify replacement properties early and adhere strictly to IRS deadlines (45 days to identify, 180 days to close).
- **Use professional management wisely.** Delegating can free your time, but make sure you still meet participation requirements if aiming for REPS.

Real estate can be both a lifestyle asset and a financial engine. Approach it with the diligence you bring to your practice, and it will reward you with income, appreciation and tax advantages.

PART III
SEEING THE WHOLE FIELD

MACRO MOVES FOR LONG TERM IMPACT

Wealth isn't built in isolation—it's orchestrated: entities, trusts, real estate, and advanced planning that work in harmony, not silos.

CHAPTER 9

❦

THE ARCHITECTURE OF PROTECTION

"Own nothing, control everything." —John D. Rockefeller

"The wealthy don't make more money; they structure it differently." —
Paavan Kotini

THE ARCHITECTURE OF PROTECTION

So far, we've talked about micro strategies-deductions, credits, and depreciation. These are the foundational tools that every doctor should be using.

But now we're going to shift gears and talk about **macro strategies**-the bigger levers that can save you six or even seven figures over your career.

These strategies require more planning, more structure, and often more upfront cost. But the payoff is enormous.

Let's start with trusts and entities– the architecture of protection.

Figure 9.1: Trusts and entity structures can protect assets, reduce taxes and coordinate wealth across generations.

* * *

WHY STRUCTURE MATTERS

Most doctors operate as individuals. They earn W-2 income, pay taxes on it, and invest what's left.

But here's the problem: **individuals are taxed at the highest rates and have the least protection.**

When you earn income as an individual:

- You're taxed at ordinary income rates (up to 37% federal, plus state)
- You have limited deduction opportunities
- Your assets are exposed to lawsuits and creditors

But when you earn income through entities (LLCs, S-corps, partnerships, trusts), you can:

- Shift income to lower tax brackets
- Create additional deduction opportunities
- Protect your assets from lawsuits

Let me show you how.

* * *

THE S-CORP STRATEGY

If you have side income (consulting, speaking, expert witness work, etc.), one of the most powerful structures you can use is an **S-corporation.**

Here's why:

When you earn self-employment income as a sole proprietor (or through a single-member LLC taxed as a sole proprietorship), you pay:

- Regular income tax (based on your bracket)
- Self-employment tax: 15.3% on net earnings (12.4% Social Security + 2.9% Medicare)

That self-employment tax hurts. On $100,000 of net self-employment income, you're paying $15,300 in self-employment tax-before income tax.

But when you structure your business as an S-corp, you can split your income into two buckets:

1. **Reasonable salary** (subject to payroll taxes)
2. **Distributions** (NOT subject to self-employment tax)

Example:

Dr. Rachel Kim earns $120,000 from medical consulting (after business expenses).

Option 1: Sole Proprietor

- Net income: $120,000
- Self-employment tax: $16,955
- Income tax (35% bracket): $42,000
- **Total tax: $58,955**

Option 2: S-Corp

- Reasonable salary: $60,000 (subject to payroll taxes)
- Distribution: $60,000 (NOT subject to self-employment tax)
- Payroll tax on salary: $9,180
- Income tax on total $120,000: $42,000
- **Total tax: $51,180**

Tax savings: $7,775 per year

Over 20 years, that's **$155,500 in savings**-just from changing the structure.

What's a "Reasonable Salary"?

The IRS requires that you pay yourself a "reasonable salary" before taking distributions. This prevents abuse (like paying yourself $1 in salary and taking $500,000 in distributions).

The rule of thumb: your salary should reflect what you'd pay someone else to do the same work. For physician consulting or expert witness work, that's typically 40-60% of net income.

When Does S-Corp Make Sense?

S-corp structure makes sense when:

- Your side business generates at least $60,000-$80,000 in net income (after expenses)
- You have consistent, ongoing business income (not just one-off projects)
- You're willing to handle additional administrative requirements (payroll, quarterly filings)

* * *

TRUSTS

A **trust** is a legal arrangement that allows one party (the *trustee*) to hold and manage assets on behalf of another (the *beneficiary*) according to terms set by the *grantor* (also called the *settlor* or *trustor*). Think of it as a financial "container" designed to protect, control, and direct the flow of wealth — both during life and after death.

Trusts can serve many purposes: minimizing taxes, protecting assets from creditors, avoiding probate, supporting loved ones, or ensuring that charitable goals are met. The flexibility lies in how the trust is structured and when it becomes effective. Below are some common types (there are more beyond this list) and why one would try to use a specific type of trust.

Primary Goal	Best-Fit Trust Type	Key Benefits	Control Level
Avoid probate and retain flexibility	**Revocable Living Trust**	Simple management, privacy	High
Reduce estate taxes and protect assets	**Irrevocable Trust**	Removes assets from estate	Low
Provide for minors or dependents after death	**Testamentary Trust**	Managed by trustee post-death	Moderate
Combine giving with lifetime income	**Charitable Remainder Trust (CRT)**	Income stream + charitable deduction	Moderate
Prioritize charity first, family later	**Charitable Lead Trust (CLT)**	Reduces estate taxes, philanthropic legacy	Low
Transfer appreciating assets tax-efficiently	**Grantor Retained Annuity Trust (GRAT)**	Minimized gift tax on appreciation	Low
Keep life insurance proceeds estate-tax free	**Irrevocable Life Insurance Trust (ILIT)**	Tax-free liquidity for heirs	Low
Support disabled loved ones	**Special Needs Trust**	Preserves government benefits	Moderate
Gift a home while retaining use	**Qualified Personal Residence Trust (QPRT)**	Reduces taxable estate value	Low
Protect heirs from creditors or overspending	**Spendthrift Trust**	Shields assets from misuse	Low–Moderate

Figure 9.2: A quick list to show the variety of trusts, their use, and level of control.

* * *

Irrevocable Life Insurance Trusts (ILITs)

Let's talk about life insurance and estate taxes.

If you own a life insurance policy when you die, the death benefit is included in your estate for estate tax purposes-even though it's income-tax-free to your beneficiaries.

Example: You have a $5 million life insurance policy. Your estate is worth $15 million. Total estate: $20 million.

If you're over the estate tax exemption ($15 million per person under OBBB), you could pay 40% estate tax on the $5 million life insurance benefit-$2 million in taxes.

The solution: An **Irrevocable Life Insurance Trust (ILIT).**

Here's how it works:

1. You create an ILIT (an irrevocable trust that you cannot control or change)
2. The ILIT purchases a life insurance policy on your life (or you transfer an existing policy to it)
3. You make annual gifts to the ILIT to cover the premium payments
4. When you die, the death benefit is paid to the ILIT-not to your estate
5. Because the ILIT owns the policy (not you), the death benefit is excluded from your estate

Tax savings: If you have a $5 million policy and you're subject to estate taxes, an ILIT could save your heirs **$2 million** (40% of $5 million).

* * *

CHARITABLE REMAINDER TRUSTS (CRTs)

Here's another powerful trust strategy: **Charitable Remainder Trusts.**

A CRT allows you to:

1. Donate an appreciated asset to charity
2. Receive income from that asset for life (or a set number of years)

3. Get an immediate tax deduction
4. Avoid capital gains tax on the sale

Here's how it works:

You transfer an appreciated asset (stock, real estate, business interest) into a CRT. The CRT sells the asset-tax-free-and invests the proceeds. You receive annual income (typically 5-8% of the trust value) for life or a term of years. When you die (or the term ends), the remaining assets go to charity.

Example: You bought stock 20 years ago for $100,000. It's now worth $1 million.

If you sold it yourself:

- Capital gains: $900,000
- Tax (23.8% federal): $214,200
- Net proceeds: $785,800

If you transfer it to a CRT:

- CRT sells stock: $1 million (no capital gains tax)
- CRT invests $1 million
- You receive 6% annual income: $60,000/year for life
- Immediate charitable deduction: ~$400,000 (present value of the remainder interest)
- Tax savings from deduction (40% bracket): $160,000

Benefits:

- You avoided $214,200 in capital gains tax
- You got a $160,000 tax deduction
- You receive $60,000/year for life (if you live 30 years, that's $1.8 million in income)
- You made a charitable gift

* * *

QUESTIONS TO THINK **About**

1. **Am I operating as an individual when I could benefit from entity structuring?** *(If you have any side income over $50,000, you should be considering an S-Corp.)*
2. **What's my net worth trajectory, and should I be thinking about estate planning now?** *(If you're on track to have a $10+ million estate, estate planning isn't optional.)*
3. **Do I have highly appreciated assets that I want to sell but am avoiding due to capital gains?** *(A CRT might be the perfect solution.)*

* * *

QUESTIONS TO ASK **Your CPA**

1. **Should I elect S-Corp status for my side business?** (They should be able to run the math and show you the potential savings vs. the administrative costs.)
2. **At what net worth should I start thinking about ILITs?** (Generally, when your net worth approaches the estate tax exemption (currently $15 million individual, $30 million married).)
3. **Do you work with an estate planning attorney? Can you coordinate on trust and entity strategies?** (This is critical. Your CPA and estate attorney need to work together.)

* * *

THE BOTTOM LINE

Trusts and entities aren't just for the ultra-wealthy. They're tools that high-income doctors should be using to:

- Reduce taxes
- Protect assets

- Transfer wealth efficiently

But they require planning. They require coordination. And they require a team.

That's what we'll talk about next.

* * *

ADDITIONAL INSIGHTS **& Action Steps**

Legal entities and trusts are the scaffolding of a durable wealth plan. They control how income flows, who pays taxes and who ultimately benefits from your hard work. The right combination can limit liability, reduce taxes and preserve privacy. An S-corporation can convert some of your income from wages (subject to payroll taxes) to distributions (which are not), while a C-corporation can provide fringe benefits and lower corporate tax rates if properly structured. Trusts like revocable living trusts ensure your assets bypass probate, whereas irrevocable trusts-such as an Irrevocable Life Insurance Trust-remove assets from your estate entirely.

Imagine **Dr. Simmons**, an orthopedic surgeon with a thriving practice. She operates through an S-corp to minimize self-employment taxes on a portion of her earnings. She also establishes a Charitable Remainder Trust (CRT) funded with appreciated stock. The CRT sells the stock tax-free, pays her an income stream for life and leaves the remainder to her favourite medical charity. Finally, she creates an Irrevocable Life Insurance Trust to own a permanent insurance policy. The death benefit will pass to her heirs outside of her estate and free of estate tax. By layering entities and trusts thoughtfully, Dr. Simmons protects her assets from malpractice claims, supports her philanthropic goals and maximizes what her family receives.

Here's how you can begin building your own structure:

- **Assess your risk.** Physicians in high-risk specialties may benefit from additional layers of protection. A malpractice claim shouldn't erase your net worth.

- **Choose the right entity for your practice.** Evaluate S-corps, C-corps and LLCs with a professional. The decision affects payroll taxes, retirement plan options and fringe benefits.
- **Incorporate trusts into your estate plan.** A revocable living trust manages your affairs during incapacity, while irrevocable trusts can remove assets from your taxable estate.
- **Coordinate with insurance.** Entities and trusts should work hand in glove with your liability, life and disability coverage.
- **Review regularly.** Laws change, your practice evolves and family dynamics shift. Conduct an annual check-up to ensure your structure still matches your goals.

The structures you build today will support your family for decades. Investing time in getting them right is one of the most generous gifts you can give your future self and your heirs.

CHAPTER 10

❧

RETIREMENT ACCOUNTS ON STEROIDS

"Do not save what is left after spending, but spend what is left after saving."
— *Warren Buffett*

"Traditional retirement planning builds a nest egg. Proactive planning builds a launchpad—one that lets your wealth keep working long after you stop."—
Paavan Kotini

RETIREMENT ACCOUNTS ON STEROIDS

❦

*M*ost doctors think they're maxing out their retirement savings because they contribute $23,500 to their 401(k) every year.

But here's the truth: **$23,500 is just scratching the surface.**

If you're a high-income doctor and you're only saving $23,500—$34,750(with catch up past age 60) a year in tax-advantaged accounts, you're leaving massive tax savings on the table.

Let me show you how to supercharge your retirement savings-and your tax deductions.

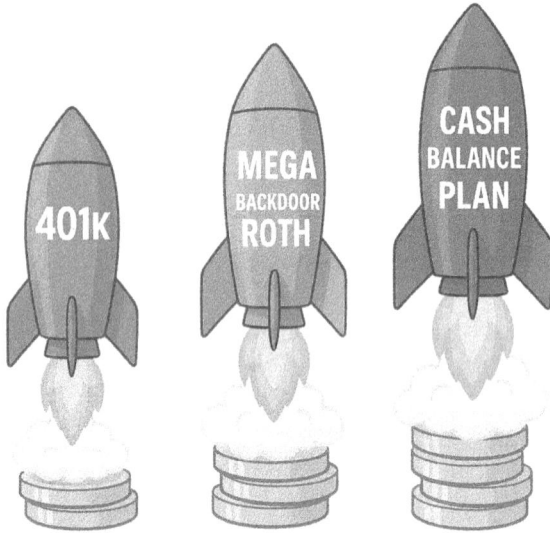

Figure 10.1: Supercharged retirement accounts like mega backdoor Roths and cash balance plans help accelerate your tax-advantaged savings.

* * *

The Retirement Savings Hierarchy

From basic building blocks to advanced deferral strategies for doctors and practice owners.

Level 1: The Foundation — 401(k) / 403(b)
Employee Contribution Limits (2025):

- Under age 50: **$23,500**
- Age 50–59 (standard catch-up): **$23,500 + $7,500 = $31,000**
- Age 60–63 (expanded "mega" catch-up under SECURE 2.0): **$23,500 + $11,250 = $34,750**

Total Employee Deferral Range: $23,500–$34,750

. . .

LEVEL 2: Add Health Savings (HSA) — The Hidden Gem
2025 HSA Contribution Limits:

- Individual coverage: **$4,300**
- Family coverage: **$8,550**
- Catch-up (age 55+): + **$1,000**

Total Retirement Savings Potential (401(k) + HSA): ≈ $27,800–$43,300

LEVEL 3: Add the Backdoor Roth IRA
For high-income earners who exceed Roth IRA income limits.

- Roth IRA (individual): **$7,000**
- Roth IRA (spouse): **$7,000**

Combined Roth Add-On: + $14,000
Total Retirement Contributions (Levels 1–3): ≈ $41,800–$57,300 per year
Tax Savings (approx. 40% bracket): ≈ $15,000–$20,000 on pre-tax contributions (401(k) + HSA)

(Roth contributions are after-tax but grow tax-free forever.)

LEVEL 4: Employer Profit Sharing / Solo 401(k)
Total Annual Limit (2025):

- **$69,000** (under 50)
- **$76,500** (age 50+)
- Employee + Employer contributions combined.

That means your employer (or your own LLC if self-employed) can contribute an **additional ~$45,500–$46,000** on top of your employee deferral.

Example: Dr. Patel (Age 45)

- Employee 401(k) contribution: **$23,500**
- Employer profit sharing: **$46,000**
- **Total:** $69,500
- **Tax savings (40% rate):** ≈ **$27,800**

If employed by a hospital or large group, your match might only be 3–5%. But if you own your own practice or side LLC, you can design your own plan and capture the full benefit.

Level 5: The Doctor's Pension — Cash Balance or Defined Benefit Plan

For practice owners or high-earning professionals who want **massive pre-tax deferrals** and consistent long-term planning.

Cash Balance Plan Contribution Range (2025):

- Typically **$100,000–$250,000+**, depending on age, income, and actuarial limits.

Example: Dr. Robert Chen (Age 50, income $500,000)

- 401(k): $31,000 (age 50+ limit)
- Profit sharing: $38,500
- Cash Balance Plan: $230,000
- **Total Retirement Contribution:** $299,500
- **Tax Savings (40% rate):** ≈ **$119,800 (Year 1)**

Over 15 years, he can **defer $4.5 million** and **save $1.8 million** in cumulative taxes—all while building a guaranteed retirement benefit.

Best for:

- Practice owners / partners
- Age 45+ high earners ($300,000+ income)
- Willing to maintain contributions for 3–5+ years

* * *

ADVANCED LEVEL: **The Mega Backdoor Roth**

If your employer 401(k) allows **after-tax contributions** up to the **total plan limit ($69,000 or $76,500)**, you can convert those after-tax dollars into Roth savings.

Example: Dr. Maria Lopez

- Employee contribution: $23,500
- Employer match: $15,000
- After-tax contributions: $31,000
- → **Total = $69,500**

She converts the $31,000 after-tax portion to a Roth 401(k), turning it into **tax-free growth for life**—far beyond the standard $7,000 IRA limit.

* * *

BONUS: **HSA — The Triple-Tax Advantage**

Often overlooked, the HSA is one of the accounts with **three tax benefits**:

1. **Tax-deductible contributions**

2. **Tax-free growth**

3. **Tax-free withdrawals for medical expenses**

2025 Contribution Limits:

- Individual: $4,300
- Family: $8,550
- Age 55+ catch-up: $1,000

Strategy:

Max out your HSA yearly but **don't spend it now**.

Pay medical expenses out of pocket and let the HSA grow. You can reimburse yourself decades later (no time limit), or use it tax-free in retirement for healthcare, Medicare, or long-term care.

Example:

Dr. Chen contributes $8,550 per year for 30 years.

At a 7% return, it grows to ~**$815,000 — completely tax-free.**

* * *

SUMMARY: **The Compounding Power of Layers**

Level	Strategy	Contribution Range	Tax Treatment
1	401(k) / 403(b)	$23,500–$34,750	Pre-tax
2	HSA	+$4,300–$8,550	Triple-tax-advantaged
3	Backdoor Roth	+$7,000–$14,000	After-tax, tax-free growth
4	Profit Sharing	+$40,000–$46,000	Employer / self-funded pre-tax
5	Cash Balance Plan	+$100,000–$250,000+	Pre-tax, defined benefit
Total Potential	**$175,000–$350,000+/yr**	**Massive current-year deferral**	

Figure 10.1: Summary showing the power of compounding layering and the type of tax treatment.

Key Takeaway:

Most doctors stop at Level 3.
True wealth acceleration begins at Level 4 and 5,
where strategy replaces limitation.

* * *

QUESTIONS TO THINK **About**

1. **What level of the retirement savings hierarchy am I currently at?** *(Most doctors are at Level 1-3. Can you get to Level 4 or 5?)*
2. **Am I leaving six figures in tax deductions on the table because I don't have the right retirement plan structure?** *(If you're a practice owner or have significant side income, probably yes.)*
3. **Is my HSA just sitting there, or am I maximizing its triple-tax advantage?** *(Most people don't realize the HSA is the best retirement account in the tax code.)*

* * *

QUESTIONS TO ASK **Your CPA**

1. **Am I maxing out all available retirement contribution opportunities?** *(They should walk you through Levels 1-5 and show you where you currently are.)*
2. **Should I consider a Cash Balance Plan or Defined Benefit Plan?** *(They should run an analysis showing potential contributions and tax savings.)*
3. **Does my 401(k) plan allow after-tax contributions and in-plan Roth conversions?** *(For the Mega Backdoor Roth strategy.)*

* * *

THE BOTTOM LINE

Most doctors think $23,000/year is the max they can save in tax-advantaged accounts.

But with the right structure, you can save $200,000 to $300,000+ per year-all tax-deductible.

That's $80,000 to $120,000 in annual tax savings.

Over a 20-year career, that's $1.6 to $2.4 million in tax savings.

So stop thinking small. Start thinking big.

* * *

ADDITIONAL INSIGHTS & Action Steps

Most physicians are familiar with 401(k)s and IRAs, but those accounts are just the tip of the retirement iceberg. Cash balance plans, defined benefit plans and the so-called mega backdoor Roth can supercharge your savings when used properly. A cash balance plan is a hybrid between a defined contribution and defined benefit plan; it allows employers (including your own S-corp) to contribute far more than the $23,000 cap on a traditional 401(k), often in excess of $200,000 depending on your age and income. Contributions are tax-deductible to the business and grow tax-deferred until distribution.

Dr. Nguyen, a radiologist nearing retirement, maxed out her 401(k) and profit-sharing plan. Yet she still had surplus cash that was being taxed at the highest rates. Her advisors set up a cash balance plan funded by her professional corporation. In three years she contributed nearly $500,000 pre-tax, dramatically reducing her taxable income while building a substantial retirement nest egg. Simultaneously, she took advantage of the mega backdoor Roth by making after-tax contributions to her 401(k) and immediately converting them to Roth dollars. She now has a pool of tax-free money that will never be subject to required minimum distributions.

To level up your retirement strategy:

- **Max out the basics first.** Ensure you are contributing to your 401(k), 403(b) or 457 plan up to the IRS limits. Take advantage of employer matches.
- **Explore advanced plans.** If you are self-employed or own your practice, investigate cash balance or defined benefit plans. They require actuarial calculations and annual funding but offer enormous deduction potential.
- **Use the mega backdoor Roth.** If your 401(k) allows after-tax contributions and in-plan conversions, you can funnel an additional $30,000–$40,000 per year into Roth accounts.
- **Coordinate with business entities.** Your choice of entity affects which retirement plans you can implement. Make sure your corporate structure and retirement strategy are aligned.
- **Plan for distributions.** A mix of taxable, tax-deferred and tax-free accounts gives you flexibility in retirement. Withdraw strategically to manage your tax bracket.

Don't let the "set it and forget it" mentality rob you of future wealth. Retirement planning is dynamic; revisiting it regularly ensures your money is working as hard as you do.

CHAPTER 11

❦

7702 —THE DOCTOR'S & DENTIST'S "ROTH"

"The wealthy buy assets. The ultra-wealthy buy time —and tax treatment."
—Anonymous

"It's not what you make. It's what you get to keep —and what keeps working for you, tax-free." —Paavan Kotini

7702 — THE DOCTOR'S & DENTIST'S "ROTH"

⚜

Why Section 7702 Matters

Most doctors and dentists know life insurance as a safety net —a necessary evil to protect their families "just in case."

But the ultra-wealthy view it as something else entirely: a living asset.

Hidden inside the tax code (Section 7702) lies one of the most flexible and powerful wealth-building tools available —one that, when structured correctly, functions like a *private Roth IRA on steroids*.

Section 7702 defines what qualifies as *life insurance* under the Internal Revenue Code. And in doing so, it gives policyholders access to one of the few remaining ways to build *tax-free* wealth outside of government limits and restrictions.

For the medical professional whose income often phases out of Roth IRA eligibility, 7702-based insurance becomes the silent partner in a lifetime of proactive tax planning, it is often known as a 'Tax-Free Roth Alternative'. Remember though, that it is an insurance vehicle to mitigate risk with tremendous tax benefits (why? Because the government is trying to incentivize you to get it!).

The Power of 7702: More Than Death Benefit

When properly designed (usually as an indexed universal life or variable universal life policy), a 7702 plan allows for:

- Tax-deferred growth on the inside buildup.

- Tax-free access through loans and withdrawals in retirement.

- Tax-free transfer to heirs through the death benefit.

That's the triple tax advantage of 7702: growth, access, and legacy —all within one vehicle.

Compare that to traditional qualified plans:

Tax Efficient Account Comparison					
Plan Type	Contribution Limits	Tax on Growth	Tax on Distribution	Access Before 59.5	Income Testing Eligibility
Roth IRA IRC §408A	$7,000/year	Tax-free	Tax-free	Restricted	Phased out above $240k
Traditional IRA IRC §408	$7,000/year	Tax-deferred	Taxed as ordinary income	Penalized unless exception applies	Deductibility phases out at higher income levels (between roughly $77,000-$240,000 depending on filing status and workplace coverage). Above those ranges, you can still contribute, but it becomes a non-deductible IRA (potentially eligible for a backdoor Roth strategy).
401(k) IRC §401(k)	$23,000/year	Tax-deferred	Taxed as ordinary income	Penalized	None
7702 Plan -CV Life Insurance IRC §7702	Flexible (hundreds of thousands)	Tax-deferred	Tax-free if accessed via policy loans	Tax-free via loans	None

Figure 11.1: This chart quickly compares common traditional plans with a 7702 plan.

For the right professional, this becomes the "wealth vault" that combines insurance, investment, and intergenerational strategy.

* * *

THREE PAYORS —One Strategy

No matter who funds the policy, the principle remains: 7702 is not about insurance *needs* but *intentional design*. Let's look at the three primary payor types:

. . .

1. Individually Owned

The most common. The doctor or dentist personally owns the policy, pays premiums, and names family members or trusts as beneficiaries. This setup builds personal tax-free income and ensures family security. It's the classic structure —but limited by one's own after-tax cash flow. Used properly, this becomes a personal retirement supplement —the "tax-free bucket" that can offset RMDs, sequence risk, or future tax hikes.

2. Business-Owned

For those who operate as S-Corps, C-Corps, or partnerships, the business can fund policies as part of *executive bonus* or *retention* plans. Here, life insurance becomes a corporate tool —deductible in some cases through bonuses, or structured for deferred compensation. It can also fund *buy-sell agreements* or serve as a *key person policy* —a safeguard for continuity when the practice itself is the asset.

3. Trust-Owned

The quiet powerhouse of multigenerational planning. When a trust (often an Irrevocable Life Insurance Trust or ILIT) owns the policy, it removes proceeds from the taxable estate. Trust-owned life insurance is the preferred tool of families seeking legacy liquidity — especially when estate values exceed exemption limits.

It's how the ultra-wealthy transfer tens of millions tax-free, generation after generation.

* * *

THREE LEVELS OF FUNDING: The 7702 Ladder

1. Self-Pay (Standard Premium)

The entry-level approach —straightforward, transparent, and flexible. You fund the policy personally or through your business. Cash value builds. You control when to access it. Think of it as a personalized Roth IRA —but with no income limits, and with death benefits attached.

2. Premium Financing

For higher earners who prefer leverage to liquidity. Here, a bank lends the funds to pay large premiums, using the policy's cash value and death benefit as collateral.

You pay only the loan interest annually —often 4–6%. When structured properly, your policy growth can exceed the interest cost, amplifying your wealth while minimizing out-of-pocket expense. Doctors and dentists with consistent income but limited liquid assets often use this as a bridge to fund large-scale policies without disrupting cash flow.

3. Premium Funded (Private Reserve Strategy)

Reserved for families and individuals with *$20 million+ in net worth*. Here, existing assets or investment portfolios fund the premiums indirectly through private arrangements or dedicated vehicles.

You don't write a check —your assets do the work. This is the ultra-high-net-worth's "no-cash Roth," where sophisticated structures create tax-free compounding without personal capital outlay. Think of it as the *Family Office Roth IRA* —without limits, without penalties, and without public visibility.

Payor Type ↓ / Funding Level →			
	Self-Pay	Premium Financed	Premium Funded
Individual	Uses after-tax dollars to build tax-free cash value and legacy protection.	Uses leverage to fund large policies with minimal out-of-pocket expense.	Family assets indirectly fund premiums for total tax-free growth.
Business	Employer or practice pays premiums as benefit or key-person coverage.	Financing enables executive-bonus or deferred-comp programs efficiently.	Corporate surplus or captive structures fund long-term wealth plans.
Trust	ILIT holds policy to remove proceeds from estate.	Financing keeps liquidity while creating inter-generational wealth transfer.	Private-trust funding strategy creates dynastic, tax-exempt family capital.

Figure 11.2: Three payors. Three funding levels. One unifying code: 7702 — the ultra-wealthy's Roth.

* * *

APPLICATIONS BEYOND RETIREMENT

A 7702-based plan is a Swiss Army knife of financial design. It touches nearly every pillar of a Virtual Family Office plan.

- Retirement Income Planning: Create a tax-free income stream in retirement that supplements qualified plans and Social Security.

- College Planning: Parents can fund policies on children to later access tax-free distributions for education —without FAFSA impact.

- Business Continuity: Serve as a funding vehicle for buy-sell or key-person insurance.

- Estate & Legacy: Transfer wealth efficiently with liquidity to pay estate taxes, ensuring heirs receive full value without forced liquidation.

- Philanthropy: Combine 7702 strategies with charitable remainder or lead trusts to magnify impact while reducing taxable estates.

* * *

Why It's the UHNW's "Roth" and why it could be your Dentist/Doctors 'Roth'

For ultra-high-net-worth families, Roth IRAs are rounding errors. Their contribution caps are irrelevant.

What they need are *tax shelters without ceilings* —and that's exactly what Section 7702 delivers.

It's how billionaires legally create tax-free dynasties.

When designed under the Modified Endowment Contract (MEC) limits, 7702 plans grow quietly, sheltered from both market volatility and government reach.

The rules haven't changed much since the 1980s —and that stability is precisely why family offices lean on them. While tax laws shift with every administration, 7702 remains one of the most resilient, court-tested corners of the Code. As a Doctor and Dentist this could be your 'Roth-like' strategy for tax free wealth. Warning: design is everything. A improperly designed may not achieve your intended goal. Design factors include, policy size, health rating, premium design, cash value/guideline testing, age, carrier, and much more. In the simplest way though if looking at funding relative to 'target' premium as insurance carriers call it you can contribute to closer to 'target' then its more like a insurance policy with cash value benefits or on the other end of the spectrum you can fund it to max 'guideline annual' and have it more like a cash value with some insurance benefits. The latter is what makes it more attractive to dentist, doctors, and UHNW families. Its efficiency of growth is exponential.

HOW PERMANENT LIFE INSURANCE WORKS (IRC 7702)

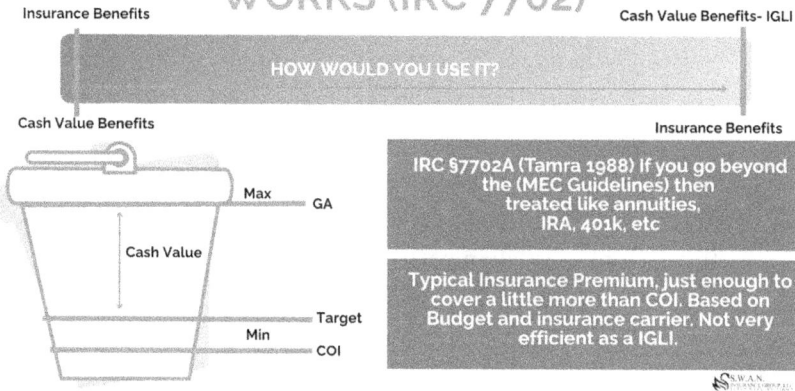

Insurance Benefits   Cash Value Benefits- IGLI

HOW WOULD YOU USE IT?

Cash Value Benefits   Insurance Benefits

Max
GA

Cash Value

IRC §7702A (Tamra 1988) If you go beyond the (MEC Guidelines) then treated like annuities, IRA, 401k, etc

Typical Insurance Premium, just enough to cover a little more than COI. Based on Budget and insurance carrier. Not very efficient as a IGLI.

Target
Min
COI

Figure 11.3: Every permanent policy carries both insurance and cash value — it's simply a matter of which one you want to work harder for you. Image Source: S.W.A.N. Insurance Group.

* * *

CLINICAL CASE: **Dr. Amara Patel**

Dr. Amara Patel, a 48-year-old oral surgeon, maxed her 401(k), funded backdoor Roths for years, and built a $10M net worth.

But she realized her tax exposure was ballooning —nearly 47% marginal combined rate.

Her Virtual Family Office designed a *premium-financed 7702 plan*: $500,000 annual premium funded via bank financing for seven years.

By age 65, she projected $280,000 per year in *tax-free retirement income* —with $6 million in tax-free death benefit for her heirs.

She didn't need more investments. She needed *tax-free control* — and Section 7702 delivered it.

* * *

QUESTIONS TO ASK **Your CPA**

1. *Am I overfunding taxable or tax-deferred accounts without building tax-free capacity?* (Balance your buckets.)

2. *Does my income phase me out of Roth eligibility?* (If yes, 7702 may be your private alternative.)
3. *Would a business—or trust-owned policy better serve my goals?* (Ownership determines control and tax treatment.)
4. *Could premium financing or funding strategies reduce my out-of-pocket costs?* (Leverage can enhance efficiency if managed well.)
5. *How does this integrate with my broader estate or exit plan?* (Every tool must align with the endgame.)

* * *

BOTTOM LINE

Section 7702 is not a loophole —it's legislation. It was designed to encourage long-term financial protection and discipline —but when optimized, it becomes a cornerstone of tax-free wealth strategy.

Doctors and dentists who embrace the S.W.A.N.™ philosophy don't just buy insurance.

They *design liquidity.*

They *own tax-free options.*

And they *build legacies that sleep well at night.*

PART IV
CASE STUDIES & THE DOCTOR'S/ DENTIST'S FAMILY OFFICE

❦

INTEGRATION TURNS INFORMATION INTO TRANSFORMATION

Real-world examples and the blueprint for building your own DFO—where advisors align, strategies synchronize, and clarity creates confidence.

CHAPTER 12

HOW DOCTORS BUILD & SELL WITHOUT SURRENDERING WEALTH

"The secret of change is to focus all of your energy not on fighting the old, but on building the new." – Socrates

"It's not always about getting the greatest sale price; it's about designing the most tax-efficient transition." – Paavan Kotini

HOW DOCTORS BUILD & SELL WITHOUT SURRENDERING WEALTH

From Ownership to Outcome

Selling a medical or dental practice is not merely a financial transaction-it's a legacy transition. You've spent decades diagnosing, leading, and healing. The final exam is not what you sell your practice for, but **how much you keep after taxes** and how efficiently those dollars continue to work for you.

A $1.5 million sale can leave you with barely $1 million after tax-or $1.5 million still compounding, tax-free. The difference lies not in valuation, but in **integration**: aligning your operating structure, risk management, and tax planning *years* before you sign the sale documents. **Your allocation is your destiny.**

Ordinary Income vs Capital Gain

Feature	W-2 Income	Ordinary Income (General)	Capital Gain
Source	Wages or salary earned as an employee	Business income, interest, short-term gains, or self-employment earnings	Profit from selling a capital asset (like stocks, real estate, or a business)
Federal Tax Rate	Marginal tax brackets (10%-37%)	Marginal tax brackets (10%-37%)	**Short-term:** Taxed at ordinary rates (10%-37%) **Long-term:** Preferential rates (0%, 15%, or 20%)
Holding Period	N/A — earned through ongoing labor	N/A	**Short-term:** Held ≤ 1 year **Long-term:** Held > 1 year
Payroll Taxes	Yes — subject to Social Security & Medicare	Yes — on earned portion only	No — but high earners may owe 3.8% Net Investment Income Tax (NIIT)

Figure 12.1: Chart comparing Ordinary income vs Capital Gain. A well-planned allocation turns a taxable event into a wealth-design opportunity.

* * *

CLINICAL CASE: **Dr. Arjun Mehta**

Dr. Arjun Mehta, 58, spent his career refining precision procedures. Two years before selling his specialty practice for $1.5 million, he began working with a Virtual Family Office-integrating tax, legal, and risk strategy.

- His **personal goodwill** was carved out and qualified as capital gain.
- He established an **831(b) micro-captive** to insure practice-specific risks-equipment downtime, key-person loss, regulatory defense, cyber liability.
- The **premiums** his operating practice paid were *deductible*, while the captive accumulated reserves tax-deferred under § 831(b).
- When Dr. Mehta sold the practice, the captive's surplus provided **liquidity for his next chapter**-funding retirement, Opportunity Zone reinvestments, or a personal foundation.

- His **capital-gain portion** from the sale was then reinvested through a qualified tax strategy, creating tax-free income and a potential tax-free multiple over 10 years.

Result: a coordinated plan that managed risk efficiently during his operating years and transformed into tax-advantaged capital at exit.

* * *

THE 831(B) ADVANTAGE: **Managing Risk While Building Wealth**

Doctors insure everything-hands, malpractice, buildings-but rarely insure *the business itself* in a way that creates value.

That's where the § 831(b) micro-captive election comes in.

How It Works

- Your operating practice forms or joins a **small insurance company** (a "micro-captive").
- The practice pays **deductible premiums** to the captive for legitimate business risks.
- The captive elects § 831(b) status, paying tax only on its investment income, not underwriting profits (subject to the current premium cap).
- Over time, **underwriting profits accumulate tax-deferred**, building an internal reserve of capital that can later be distributed, reinsured, or repurposed in succession planning.

Why It Matters

- **Risk Management:** Provides tailored coverage unavailable or uneconomical in the commercial market.
- **Tax Efficiency:** Converts nondeductible retained earnings into deductible premiums.
- **Exit Amplifier:** The captive can serve as a **pre-funded**

transition vehicle, providing liquidity for buy-outs, retirement income, or even intergenerational transfers.
- **Legacy Structuring:** Properly designed, the captive can dovetail with trusts, Opportunity Zones, or charitable entities for long-term compounding.

(Captives must meet IRS standards for risk shift, risk distribution, and insurance legitimacy. Professional guidance is essential.)

* * *

OPPORTUNITY ZONES: The Deferral Companion

Opportunity Zones remain a valuable complement to exit strategy, allowing reinvested gains to **defer taxes** and eliminate tax on future growth if held for 10 years. Yet not all OZs are created equal (discussed more in chapter 7). Underwrite them as you would any clinical device-if you wouldn't implant it without imaging, don't invest without due diligence.

Investment Category	Typical Use Case
Real Estate Development	Medical Buildings, Mixed-Use
Operating Business (QOZB)	Clinics, Asc Groups, Manufacturing
Energy & Infrastructure	Renewable Energy, Oil & Gas
Multi-Asset Funds	Diversified Oz Portfolios

Figure 12.2: While Opportunity Zones come in many forms, a tax incentive alone doesn't guarantee success. The underlying business model and the integrity of the sponsor remain the true determinants of performance.

* * *

DOCTOR'S EXIT **Checklist**
(For practice sales, mergers, or retirement transitions)

- **Entity & Allocation Review**
- Confirm your entity type (S-Corp, C-Corp, or LLC) and ensure your ownership, goodwill, and asset allocations are optimized for tax efficiency before a sale.
- **Capital vs. Ordinary Income Mapping**
- Model the transaction to distinguish capital gains (favorable rates) from ordinary income. Strategic allocation can often reduce effective taxes by six figures.
- **831(b) Captive Feasibility Analysis**
- Assess whether a micro-captive structure can help manage pre-sale risks, create deductible reserves, and smooth post-sale cash flow under the updated OBBBA compliance standards.
- **Advanced Tax Mitigation Strategy**
- Evaluate current-law opportunities—such as **Qualified Opportunity Zones (QOZs), Charitable Remainder Trusts (CRTs)**, or structured installment sales—to defer or reduce recognized gains.
- **Pre-Sale Retirement Load-Up & Deferral Planning**
- Maximize contributions to defined benefit, cash balance, or deferred compensation plans before closing. Leverage the permanent **23% QBI deduction** and **100% bonus depreciation** where applicable.
- **Post-Sale Income, Legacy & Liquidity Structuring**
- Design your next phase: income draw strategy, family trust or foundation funding, and coordinated estate planning under the new **$15 million per-person exemption**.

* * *

Questions to Think About

1. **How much of your practice's value depends on you—and how much on systems someone else can scale?** (*If your value is personality-driven rather than process-driven, buyers pay less and risk rises.*)

2. **Could an 831(b) captive allow you to manage risks more profitably while reducing annual tax drag?** (*Captives turn unpredictable expenses into predictable, deductible premiums—reducing tax and improving control.*)

3. **Would you rather sell your practice or transition it while your captive continues generating income?** (*Structuring the exit so your captive remains active can create post-sale passive income and continuity.*)

4. **Are you selling for liquidity or for liberation?** (*Clarifying motive determines whether to optimize for cash, control, or peace of mind.*)

5. **What's your post-sale mission—wealth accumulation, philanthropy, or legacy creation?** (*Knowing your "why" shapes the tools—trusts, foundations, or family offices—you'll need afterward.*)

* * *

Questions to Ask Your CPA

1. **How will my sale be taxed—capital gain or ordinary income?** (*The answer defines whether your effective rate is closer to 20% or 37%—a six-figure difference.*)
2. **Can we shift value toward goodwill or personal assets to**

lower my tax rate? (*Allocating more of the sale price to goodwill can qualify income for lower capital gains treatment.*)

3. **Could an 831(b) micro-captive help me manage risk tax-efficiently and pre-fund part of my exit?** (*A well-structured captive can both mitigate risk and accumulate reserves that become post-sale assets.*)

4. **Are we leveraging Opportunity Zones, installment sales, or charitable trusts to defer or eliminate tax?** (*These advanced structures can spread or erase taxes while aligning with long-term goals.*)

5. **Should we restructure the entity before sale (S-Corp vs. C-Corp vs. LLC)?** (*The entity you sell from can determine your tax outcome more than the price you sell for.*)

6. **What pre-sale deductions or deferrals should I execute this year while I still control the practice?** (*Timing key deductions before closing can preserve tens of thousands in after-tax value.*)

* * *

THE BOTTOM LINE

Most doctors negotiate the sale price. The elite ones negotiate what they *keep.*

A successful exit isn't about cashing out; it's about **converting years of practice into decades of freedom**. Begin exit planning 3 – 5 years before sale with the goal: sell once, exit forever.

The 831(b) structure allows you to protect what you've built along the way. Opportunity Zones and capital-gain planning ensure your after-tax proceeds keep working. Together, they turn your exit into an evolution-where your money continues to practice long after you've retired.

ADDITIONAL INSIGHTS **& Action Steps**

1. **Run a Risk and Tax Scan.** Identify uninsured or self-insured exposures-these are candidates for an 831(b) structure.

2. **Establish Early.** Captives require seasoning. Set up 2 – 3 years before sale so premiums and reserves are established and defendable.

3. **Integrate With Exit Vehicles.** At sale, evaluate how captive surplus can fund buy-out, deferred-comp plan, or post-sale Opportunity Zone reinvestment.

4. **Stay Compliant.** Maintain arm's-length underwriting, diversify risks, and follow annual filing requirements.

5. **Visualize the Transfer.** Map your flow: Operating Practice → 831(b) Captive → Liquidity at Exit → Tax-Advantaged Reinvestment → Legacy Trust.

6. **Measure Peace of Mind.** A captively insured, tax-optimized exit is not just efficient-it's elegant.

"Operate wisely, exit gracefully, and let your money continue to heal others long after you've hung up the coat."
- Paavan Kotini

CHAPTER 13

❧

THE JOURNEY OF TWO DOCS (PART II)

"The best way to predict your future is to create it."— Peter Drucker

"Money follows intention. When you plan with precision and purpose, wealth stops being random — it becomes repeatable." — Paavan Kotini

THE JOURNEY OF TWO DOCS
(PART II)

*L*et's check back in with Dr. Michael Anderson and Dr. Arjun Mehta-the two doctors we met in Chapter 2.

Figure 13.1: Choosing proactive planning over reactive filing dramatically changes your financial trajectory.

* * *

YEAR 15: The Paths Diverge Further

Dr. Michael Anderson continues his pattern. He earns $350,000, pays $95,000 in taxes, saves what's left, and invests in a standard portfolio.	Dr. Arjun Mehta has been executing his strategy consistently:
His net worth at Year 15: **$1.8 million**	• He now owns three rental properties worth $2.5 million combined
He's doing fine. He's not in financial trouble. But he's also not building wealth as efficiently as he could be	• His consulting business generates $100,000 annually
	• He's contributed $1.5 million to his Cash Balance Plan
	• His IUL policy has $450,000 in cash value
	• He's saved $1.2 million in taxes over 15 years
	His net worth at Year 15: **$4.2 million**

Same income. Same career. But Arjun is $2.4 million ahead.

YEAR 30: Retirement

<table>
<tr>
<td>

Dr. Michael Anderson retires with:

- 401(k): $1.8 million
- Brokerage account: $800,000
- Home equity: $400,000
- **Total net worth: $3 million**

He'll have a comfortable retirement. Social Security plus withdrawals from his 401(k) will provide about $120,000 per year in income. He'll pay taxes on those withdrawals, leaving him with about $85,000 after-tax.

Not bad. But he'll always wonder what could have been if he'd planned differently.

</td>
<td>

Dr. Arjun Mehta retires with:

- 401(k): $1.8 million
- Cash Balance Plan: $2.3 million
- Rental properties (equity): $1.2 million
- IUL policy (cash value): $900,000
- Brokerage account: $1.8 million
- **Total net worth: $8 million**

His retirement income strategy:

- Rental property cash flow: $60,000/year (tax-advantaged)
- Tax-free loans from IUL: $40,000/year
- Social Security: $40,000/year
- Strategic withdrawals from tax-deferred accounts: $20,000/year
- **Total income: $160,000/year**

Because he built multiple income streams and diversified his tax treatment, his effective tax rate in retirement is only 10%-even though he's withdrawing $160,000 per year.

</td>
</tr>
</table>

* * *

30-YEAR COMPARISON: The Final Tally

Dr. Michael Anderson (The Filer):

- Total earnings: $10.5 million
- Total taxes paid: $2.85 million
- Net worth at retirement: $3 million
- Annual retirement income: $85,000 (after-tax)

Dr. Arjun Mehta (The Planner):

- Total earnings: $10.5 million
- Total taxes paid: $1.65 million
- Net worth at retirement: $8 million
- Annual retirement income: $144,000 (after-tax)

. . .

The difference:

- $1.2 million less in lifetime taxes
- $5 million more in net worth
- $59,000 more in annual retirement income

And remember: this wasn't because Arjun earned more. It wasn't because he got lucky. It was because he planned.

What Made the Difference?

Let's break down the specific strategies that created the $5 million gap:

Years 1-10:

- Side business LLC: $50,000 in tax savings
- Cost segregation on rental property: $70,000 in tax savings
- Solar tax credit: $15,000 in tax savings
- **Subtotal: $135,000**

Years 11-20:

- Cash Balance Plan contributions: $350,000 in tax savings
- Second rental property with cost segregation: $80,000 in tax savings
- IUL policy (tax-free growth): avoided $60,000 in future taxes
- 1031 exchange: deferred $90,000 in capital gains taxes
- **Subtotal: $580,000**

Years 21-30:

- Continued Cash Balance Plan: $400,000 in tax savings

- Third rental property: $100,000 in tax savings
- Leveraged charitable donations: $85,000 in tax savings
- Micro-captive insurance: $120,000 in tax savings
- **Subtotal: $705,000**

Total tax savings over 30 years: $1,420,000

BUT REMEMBER: it's not just about the tax savings. It's about what you do with those savings. Arjun reinvested his tax savings, letting them compound over 30 years. That's how $1.4 million in tax savings turned into $5 million in additional wealth.

* * *

THE LESSON

The difference between Michael and Arjun wasn't intelligence, work ethic, or luck.

It was intentionality.

Michael reacted. Arjun planned.

Michael filed. Arjun strategized.

Michael hoped. Arjun executed.

You've seen the math. You've seen the strategies. You've seen the results.

Now it's time to decide: which doctor will you be?

* * *

ADDITIONAL INSIGHTS & Action Steps

When we revisit the two fictional doctors from earlier in the book, the divergence in their outcomes becomes even more striking. **Dr. Filer** continued down the path of reactive tax preparation-delivering quarterly estimated payments, paying his April tax bill and hoping for a refund. He ignored entity structuring, skipped depreciation studies and dismissed the idea of a side business as a distraction.

After 30 years he amassed $3 million in savings, exhausted and wondering where all the money went. His stress level never abated because he never felt in control.

Dr. Planner, on the other hand, assembled a multidisciplinary team: tax advisor, wealth manager, attorney and insurance specialist. He met with them quarterly, reviewed key metrics and adjusted his strategy as his practice and family grew. He launched a tele-consulting company, invested in a handful of rentals and implemented a cash balance plan in his S-corp. At retirement he had over $8 million saved, plus income streams from real estate and dividends. More importantly, he had peace of mind because he knew his decisions were purposeful.

Reflect on how you can shift your own trajectory:

- **Establish your advisory board.** Identify trusted professionals who will collaborate rather than compete. Hold regular strategy sessions, not just year-end reviews.
- **Create key performance indicators (KPIs).** Track metrics like effective tax rate, savings rate, debt ratio and investment growth. What gets measured gets managed.
- **Commit to ongoing education.** Attend workshops, read books and stay curious. A single insight could save you six figures over your career.
- **Decide on your next move.** Whether it's forming an entity, buying a property or opening a retirement plan, schedule the first step within the next two weeks. Action begets clarity.

Your story is still being written. Will you be the filer who accepts the status quo or the planner who designs a legacy? The choice, and the path, is entirely yours.

CHAPTER 14

❧

#1 PRECRIPTION FOR TAX AND WEALTH GENERATION—THE DFO (DOCTOR'S/ DENTIST'S FAMILY OFFICE)

"Alone we can do so little; together we can do so much." —Helen Keller

"In medicine, no one heals alone. In finance, no one should plan alone." — Paavan Kotini

#1 PRECRIPTION FOR TAX AND WEALTH GENERATION—THE DFO (DOCTOR'S/ DENTIST'S FAMILY OFFICE)

We've covered a lot of strategies-deductions, credits, depreciation, trusts, retirement accounts, real estate.

But here's the thing: **strategies alone aren't enough.**

You need a system. You need a team. You need what the ultra-wealthy have had for decades: a **family office.**

Now, I'm not talking about a literal family office with a staff of 20 people managing billions of dollars. I'm talking about the **mindset** and **structure** of a family office-adapted for high-income doctors.

Let me explain.

What Is a Family Office?

A traditional family office is a private wealth management firm that serves a single ultra-high-net-worth family (typically $100 million+ in net worth).

The family office coordinates:

- Investment management
- Tax planning
- Estate planning
- Philanthropic planning
- Bill pay and administrative tasks

- Concierge services

The key concept: **everything is coordinated.**

Your investment advisor talks to your CPA. Your CPA talks to your estate attorney. Your estate attorney talks to your insurance specialist. Everyone is working together toward your financial goals.

Compare that to most doctors' situations:

- You have a financial advisor who manages your investments
- You have a CPA who files your taxes
- You have an attorney who did your will 10 years ago
- You have an insurance agent who sold you a life insurance policy
- **None of them talk to each other**

That's not planning. That's chaos.

THE DOCTOR'S FAMILY OFFICE

Figure 14.1: A coordinated family office aligns tax, investment, legal and lifestyle decisions for doctor families. When was the last time you had your legal, tax, and wealth team all talking together?

* * *

THE TALE of Two Doctors

Let me tell you about two doctors who took very different approaches to coordinating their finances.

Dr. Michael Rodriguez: The DIY Coordinator

Michael had always been hands-on. "I didn't get through medical school by letting other people do the work," he told his wife over dinner one evening. "I can figure this out."

He started by making a list of his current team:

- Tom, his CPA who he saw every April
- Jennifer, his financial advisor at a big firm
- Bob, the attorney who'd drafted his will five years ago
- Rick, his insurance agent
- His banker at Chase
- A real estate agent he'd used twice

Michael scheduled individual meetings with each of them. Tom suggested some tax strategies. Jennifer proposed a new investment allocation. Bob mentioned he should update his estate plan. Rick tried to sell him more life insurance.

Every month, Michael spent hours trying to coordinate everything. He'd get advice from Tom about tax strategies, then call Jennifer to see if they fit his investment plan. She'd suggest something different. Then he'd email Bob to ask if it affected his estate plan. Bob would bill him $400 for a 15-minute response.

By March, Michael had:

- Three different spreadsheets tracking various strategies
- A folder of conflicting advice
- A growing sense of frustration
- No implemented strategies

"When did you last operate on a patient?" his wife asked one Saturday morning, finding him at the kitchen table surrounded by financial documents.

"Thursday," he said, distracted.

"And how many hours have you spent this week trying to coordinate your finances?"

Michael looked up. "I don't know... maybe eight?"

"You could've done six surgeries in that time."

He'd saved nothing in taxes. He'd made no progress on his estate plan. And he was exhausted.

Dr. Sarah Chen: The DFO Approach

Sarah took a different path. She called Kotini & Kotini.

"I'm a surgeon," she told them in the initial consultation. "I'm good at fixing shoulders and knees. I'm not good at coordinating financial professionals, and frankly, I don't want to be."

Within two weeks, the DFO had:

- Audited her existing team
- Identified that her CPA was purely reactive and her financial advisor had never spoken to her attorney
- Assembled a coordinated team of specialists
- Scheduled a comprehensive planning meeting

At that first meeting, Sarah sat at her dining room table with her laptop while five professionals discussed her situation on a video call. The DFO quarterback facilitated everything.

"Sarah," the quarterback said, "based on your income and the surgical center sale, we've identified four strategies that could save you $127,000 in taxes this year. Your CPA has confirmed the tax treatment, your financial advisor has confirmed how it affects your investments, and your attorney has confirmed the legal structure. We just need your approval to implement."

Sarah blinked. "That's it? You already coordinated everything?"

"That's our job," the quarterback smiled. "You focus on surgery. We focus on this."

The whole meeting took 90 minutes. Sarah approved the strategies. The team implemented everything over the next three weeks. The quarterback sent her a summary document and scheduled a follow-up for three months later.

Sarah's cost: $35,000 annually for the coordinated team.

Sarah's tax savings that first year: $127,000.

Her time investment: Four hours total.

One Year Later

Michael eventually implemented some tax strategies-after spending roughly 80 hours coordinating between his various professionals. He saved about $35,000 in taxes. But he'd missed several surgical days due to the stress and distraction. His marriage was strained from the constant financial anxiety. And he'd developed a habit of waking up at 2 AM worrying about whether his CPA and financial advisor were giving him conflicting advice.

"The worst part," he confided to a colleague, "isn't even the money. It's that I'm not focusing on what I'm actually good at. I spent more time last quarter managing my financial team than I spent on continuing medical education."

Sarah, meanwhile, had her quarterly check-in call. It lasted 30 minutes. The DFO quarterback walked her through the progress on each strategy, identified two new opportunities based on recent tax law changes, and asked if anything in her life had changed that might affect their planning.

"Actually," Sarah said, "I'm thinking about cutting back to four days a week next year."

"Great," the quarterback responded. "That changes your tax picture significantly. We'll model that out and have recommendations for you by next month. It might actually create an opportunity for a deferred compensation strategy."

After the call, Sarah went for a run, picked up her kids from school, and spent the evening teaching her daughter to make pasta from scratch. She didn't think about her finances again until the next quarterly meeting.

* * *

WHAT a DFO Actually Does

A Doctor's/ Dentist's Family Office (DFO) isn't just about having multiple advisors. It's about having those advisors work as a coordinated team under a proactive planning team that acts like a quarterback.

Figure 14.2: Your Doctor's/Dentist's Family Office (DFO) begins with clarity. Together, we first **understand and prioritize your needs**, then **address your biggest problems**, and finally **help you achieve your most important goals** —all through your **Proactive Planning Team**, seamlessly coordinating every specialist around you. Source: Kotini & Kotini

Here's an example what that looks like in practice:

1. Advanced Tax Planning

Not just filing taxes-engineering tax efficiency across your entire financial life. A DFO tax team:

- Models multiple scenarios
- Identifies opportunities proactively
- Coordinates with your other advisors
- Implements strategies before year-end (not after)

2. Wealth Management & Investments

Not just investment management-building wealth aligned with your medical career and life goals. A DFO wealth team:

- Analyzes your complete balance sheet (including practice equity)
- Creates tax-aware investment strategies
- Coordinates with your tax planning
- Adjusts based on your career stage

3. Risk Management

Not just buying insurance-building comprehensive protection. A DFO risk team:

- Conducts a seven-category risk audit
- Identifies gaps and overlaps
- Coordinates policy ownership with estate planning
- Reviews coverage as your life changes

4. Practice & Business Advisory

Not just business consulting-strategic guidance for every stage of your medical career. A DFO practice team:

- Reviews employment contracts
- Analyzes partnership buy-in opportunities
- Plans for succession
- Optimizes practice structure

5. Family Governance & Legacy Planning

Not just estate planning-building multi-generational wealth and values. A DFO family team:

- Creates family governance structures
- Educates the next generation
- Coordinates philanthropic strategy
- Plans for wealth transfer

The Coordination Difference

Here's a real example of how coordination creates value:

Dr. Jennifer Walsh received a $1.5 million bonus from her hospital system.

Traditional approach: Jennifer would call five different advisors and get five different answers, none of which considered the others' advice.

DFO approach: Jennifer scheduled one meeting. Her quarterback brought together her tax advisor, wealth manager, and estate attorney. They presented one integrated recommendation:

Tax:

- Contribute $200,000 to a cash balance plan (immediate $74,000 tax savings)
- Make $50,000 in charitable contributions via donor-advised fund (additional $18,500 savings)
- Defer $150,000 in bonus to 2026 when income may be lower (potential $25,000 savings)
- **Total tax savings: $117,500**

Wealth:

- Invest $600,000 in diversified portfolio outside of healthcare sector
- Use $200,000 to fund 529 plans for children
- Keep $350,000 in liquid reserves for practice expansion opportunity

Estate:

- Update estate plan to reflect increased net worth
- Transfer $500,000 to irrevocable trust
- Update beneficiary designations

Insurance:

- Increase term life insurance by $2 million
- Structure premium payments to maximize tax efficiency

Total coordination time: One 90-minute meeting **Result:** One comprehensive strategy where every piece reinforced the others **Value delivered:** $117,500 in tax savings + optimized wealth structure + comprehensive protection

"This is the first time in my career," Jennifer said, "where I didn't leave a financial meeting more confused than when I started."

* * *

THE SLEEP WELL At Night Standard

Our ultimate measure of success isn't returns, tax savings, or account balances. It's whether you **Sleep Well At Night.**

Can you answer "yes" to these questions?

- If something happened to me tomorrow, would my family know exactly what to do?
- Am I confident I'm not overpaying taxes by six figures annually?
- If I were sued for malpractice, are my personal assets protected?
- Is my practice structured to maximize value when I eventually exit?
- Am I building wealth in a tax-efficient way aligned with my goals?
- Do I have a coordinated team handling my finances, or am I the coordinator?
- Can I focus on practicing medicine without constant financial stress?

If you answered "no" or "I'm not sure" to any of these, you need coordination. You need a quarterback. You need a DFO.

* * *

QUESTIONS TO THINK **About**

1. **Do I have a coordinated team, or do I have isolated professionals who don't talk to each other?** *(Be honest-this is where most doctors fall short.)*
2. **Am I spending $20,000/year on professionals but getting $5,000 in value-or spending $20,000 and getting $200,000 in value?** *(ROI is what matters, not absolute cost.)*
3. **If I built a truly coordinated team, how much could I save in taxes over the next 20 years?** *(For most doctors earning $400,000+, the answer is seven figures.)*

* * *

QUESTIONS TO ASK **Your Team**

1. Ask your CPA: Would you be willing to participate in an annual planning meeting with my financial advisor and attorney? *(If they say no or seem resistant, that's a red flag.)*
2. Ask your financial advisor: Do you coordinate with my CPA on tax-efficient investment strategies? *(If they don't know who your CPA is, that's a problem.)*
3. Ask your attorney: When was the last time you talked to my CPA about my estate plan? *(If they've never talked, your estate plan might not be tax-optimized.)*

* * *

THE BOTTOM LINE

Strategies are powerful. But coordinated strategies are transformational.

You didn't become a doctor by working alone. You worked with a team-attendings, residents, nurses, specialists.

Your finances should work the same way.

Build your family office. Build your team. And watch your wealth grow.

* * *

ADDITIONAL INSIGHTS & **Action Steps**

A Doctor's/ Dentist's Family Office (DFO) isn't just a fancy term; it's the operating system for your financial life. At its best a DFO functions like the command centre in a hospital-coordinating specialists, monitoring vital signs and anticipating complications before they arise. When you integrate tax strategy, investment management, legal planning and lifestyle concierge services under one roof, you reduce friction and increase clarity. No more chasing down half answers from disconnected advisors or discovering after the fact that one decision sabotaged another.

For example, **Dr. Martinez**, a cardiologist, once had separate advisors for taxes, investments and insurance who rarely spoke to one another. By transitioning to a virtual DFO, she consolidated oversight. Her CPA flagged an opportunity to implement a defined benefit plan; the investment advisor aligned asset allocation to fund that liability; the attorney updated her estate documents to reflect the new retirement accounts; and the concierge service handled the paperwork. She saved time, reduced stress and captured savings that would have otherwise fallen through the cracks.

To build or engage your own DFO, consider these steps:

- **Map your advisors.** List your CPA, financial planner, attorney, insurance agent and any other professionals. Are they communicating?
- **Define your objectives.** Clarify what success looks like-lower taxes, more free time, charitable impact or all of the above. Share this vision with your team.
- **Choose a quarterback.** Every team needs a leader who

coordinates efforts. This could be you, a family office advisor or a trusted confidante.

- **Leverage technology.** Use secure portals, shared calendars and dashboards to keep everyone on the same page.
- **Review quarterly.** The DFO model isn't a set-it-and-forget-it approach. Quarterly check-ups keep your plan aligned with your evolving life.

Your career thrives on collaboration. Apply the same philosophy to your finances and you'll find your DFO gives you the bandwidth to focus on what you love-practicing medicine and enjoying life.

CHAPTER 15

⚮

HEALTH IS WEALTH

"He who has health has hope; and he who has hope has everything." — *Thomas Carlyle*

"'You can't build wealth if your foundation, your body is bankrupt." — *Paavan Kotini*

HEALTH IS WEALTH

⚜

*T*he Wake-Up Call

It wasn't too long ago. I felt unstoppable. I was running multiple companies, managing a growing team, taking care of my family, and at least on paper living the dream.

The road had been long and challenging, but I felt I could conquer anything. Then, one ordinary morning, everything changed.

After dropping my daughter off at school, I headed toward my office. Then—BOOM. Out of nowhere, I was T-boned by a man pulling out of Dunkin' Donuts. Later, I learned he had spilled his coffee and, in a moment of panic, slammed on the accelerator instead of the brake. He hit me square on the driver's side —in my brand-new Model X.

The adrenaline took over. My mind was racing through my to-do list: meetings, calls, client deliverables. But the car wasn't going anywhere. The front axle was bent, the frame distorted. Totaled. I thought I was fine. I told myself I had to be fine.

But as the adrenaline wore off, reality set in. The aches started. Then the pain. And, worst of all, a creeping sense of confusion.

* * *

THE INVISIBLE WOUNDS

After visits to the ER and my primary care physician, the diagnosis came in pieces: physical therapy for the back, concussion therapy for the brain injury, speech therapy to help with cognition. I couldn't even read without losing focus or forgetting what I had just read. I was in tears when my elementary school daughter asked me to read a book to her to fall asleep and I couldn't do it.

Companies I had built from scratch began to falter. I'd forget conversations, deadlines—even that some of the companies existed at all. It was terrifying.

The mind that once processed complex tax structures, financial models, and strategic plans now struggled to process simple sentences.

I felt broken —not just physically, but emotionally and spiritually.

* * *

WHEN THE BODY Speaks

Over the next couple of years, I did what I was told: therapy, rehab, supplements. I got some of my bearings back, but something was still off. My energy was low. I developed diabetes, kidney stones, and vitiligo.

My doctors ran the usual tests—blood sugar, cholesterol, basic panels—and kept telling me, "Everything looks fine."

But I knew I wasn't fine.

So, I searched. I tried everything—Western medicine, Ayurveda, homeopathy, meditation. Some helped for a while. But I wanted answers, not temporary relief.

Then, one day, I met Dr. Tracy Gapin (wrote the foreward for this book).

* * *

REDEFINING Health

Dr. Gapin's story sounded eerily familiar. He too had experienced physical breakdown and frustration with traditional medicine. But instead of accepting the surface-level answers, he dug deeper—into functional and performance medicine.

He taught me something profound: how we measure health determines what we see.

Most doctors measure *total* testosterone, for example. But that's only part of the story. *Free* testosterone—the bioavailable form—is what drives energy, focus, and vitality. And it often paints a very different picture.

We're conditioned to treat symptoms, not systems. To manage illness, not optimize wellness.

Health, I realized, isn't the absence of disease. It's the presence of vitality.

* * *

THE TURNING POINT

Today, I'm still on that journey. I track my data. I run advanced panels. I look at my body like I look at a business —every metric tells a story.

I'm rebuilding from the inside out.

And as I've learned, you can't separate health from wealth. You can't make clear decisions, lead a team, or enjoy your success if your body is running on empty.

So if you're reading this and you've been putting off your own health—don't.

Alongside your tax plan and financial plan, develop your *health plan*. It's all connected.

Because when your body thrives, your business & wealth follows.

* * *

THE BOTTOM LINE

We often say "health is wealth," but it's more than a catchy phrase. It's literal. The greatest returns come from the smallest deposits you make into your own vitality—daily movement, mindful nutrition, stress management, deep sleep, and meaningful purpose.

True wealth isn't just the balance in your bank. It's the energy you bring to your life, your family, and your mission.

Because when health declines, everything else follows. But when it flourishes, everything expands.

* * *

QUESTIONS TO THINK About

1. **When was the last time you got a full health assessment —not just basic labs, but hormone, micronutrient, and metabolic testing?** (*You can't improve what you don't measure.*)
2. **If your body were a business, what would your KPIs be?** (*Energy, sleep, strength, clarity—track them.*)
3. **What habits drain your health account the fastest?** (*Poor sleep, stress, neglect—identify your biggest culprits.*)
4. **What would it look like to integrate health planning into your wealth planning?** (*Imagine your VFO includes your vitality.*)
5. **What one small action can you take today to upgrade your health trajectory?** (*Small steps compound, just like interest.*)

* * *

CLOSING Thought

The car accident totaled more than a vehicle—it totaled my illusion of invincibility.

But it also gave me something far greater: perspective.

If money is a tool for freedom, health is the fuel. One without the other leaves you stranded.

And I refuse to run out of gas again.

Health is wealth. Always.

CHAPTER 16

⤬

WHAT IS YOUR RELATIONSHIP WITH MONEY

"Money is only a tool. It will take you wherever you wish, but it will not replace you as the driver." —Ayn Rand

"You don't have to love money to respect it. You just have to understand it well enough to put it to work, ethically, efficiently, and intentionally." — Paavan Kotini

WHAT IS YOUR RELATIONSHIP
WITH MONEY

⚮

The Unspoken Relationship
Everyone has a relationship with money, whether we acknowledge it or not.

Some were born with abundance, others with scarcity, and most of us fall somewhere in between. Yet the amount we start with rarely determines where we end up. What truly shapes our relationship with money is what we learned about it: the stories we heard, the lessons we absorbed, and the patterns we repeated.

Maybe you grew up hearing "money doesn't grow on trees."

Maybe you watched your parents fight about it.

Maybe you were taught that talking about it was taboo.

Or maybe you were told that success was measured by how much you could earn and how fast.

Those early experiences became the scripts that guide how we earn, spend, save, invest, and even give.

* * *

Love It, Hate It, or Fear It

For some, money is a love story, something to be pursued passionately, counted often, and used as a scorecard.

For others, it is a source of pain, the root of conflict, inequality, or greed.

And for many, it is a ghost, something they ignore out of fear, shame, or misunderstanding.

But money itself is none of those things.

Money is neutral.

It is an instrument, not an idol.

A means, not an end.

It has no moral weight until it is placed in human hands. It simply amplifies who you already are.

If you are generous, it helps you give more.

If you are disciplined, it helps you grow more.

If you are careless, it magnifies the consequences.

No matter your relationship with money, it begins with your beliefs, which shape your feelings and, in turn, drive your behaviors.

YOUR RELATIONSHIP
WITH MONEY

Figure 16.1: Your relationship with money runs deeper than numbers. At the core lie your **beliefs**, which shape your **feelings**, which drive your **behaviors**. Transforming your financial life starts not with a new strategy, but with a new story about money itself.

* * *

MONEY AS ENERGY

Think of money as energy, constantly in motion.

It flows toward those who respect it, understand it, and direct it with purpose.

When you fear it, dismiss it, or misunderstand it, that energy dissipates. When you align with it by learning how to earn it strategically, protect it intelligently, and grow it responsibly, it multiplies.

This is not mysticism; it is mindset.

Our beliefs dictate our behaviors. If we believe money is scarce, we act reactively. If we believe it is abundant and directional, we plan proactively.

* * *

CLINICAL CASE: **Dr. Maya Patel**

Dr. Maya Patel, a pediatric dentist, was brilliant in her craft but exhausted by her finances.

Every April, she dreaded tax season, not because of paperwork, but because of what it represented: another year of working hard, earning well, and watching nearly half her income vanish.

She would sigh and say, "It is what it is. I guess that's just how the system works."

Until one day, her advisor challenged that belief.

"What if it doesn't have to be that way?" he asked. "What if mitigating taxes isn't just your right, it's your responsibility?"

That question shifted everything.

Maya began to view the tax code not as a punishment, but as a roadmap, a guide to where the government wants wealth to flow. She learned that by investing in her practice, funding employee benefits, setting up the right entity structures, and using tax-favored tools like 401(k)s, defined benefit plans, and insurance strategies, she could keep more of what she earned, all within the rules.

Within two years, Maya was not just saving on taxes. She was saving with purpose.

She hired more staff, expanded her clinic, and established a scholarship fund for aspiring dental students in her community.

What changed was not her income, it was her relationship with money.

She moved from frustration to stewardship. From passive taxpayer to proactive wealth designer.

* * *

MITIGATING TAXES: **A Civic Responsibility**

Here is where most people get it wrong.

Mitigating taxes is not cheating the system. It is understanding the system.

In a way, it is your civil responsibility to be an informed steward of your own resources. The tax code is not designed to punish success; it is designed to reward participation.

When you take advantage of tax incentives by creating jobs, investing in your business, or supporting charitable causes, you are aligning your actions with national priorities.

When you learn how to legally and ethically keep more of what you earn, you are not just protecting your wealth. You are positioning yourself to do more good with it.

You can reinvest in your practice, support your staff, fund your child's education, or build a foundation that outlives you.

Tax mitigation done right is not greed. It is good stewardship. It is using the rules as they were written, not as they are feared.

* * *

RESPECT, **Not Worship**

Respect money, but do not worship it.

It is meant to serve you, not the other way around.

Chasing money for its own sake often leads to anxiety or emptiness. But using it intentionally, to buy back time, create opportunity, and enable freedom, is where money transforms from pressure into possibility.

There is more to life than money. We all know that, yet it bears repeating. Because money has a way of making us forget what it is really for.

Money cannot buy love, health, or meaning, but it can buy space, security, and freedom to focus on them. That is the real currency of wealth: peace of mind.

* * *

REDEFINING **the Relationship**

So, what is your relationship with money?

Is it driven by fear or freedom? Scarcity or stewardship?

You do not need to be born wealthy to build wealth. You simply need to rewrite your story.

When you see money as a tool, a form of energy to be channeled, you take back control.

When you use it wisely, grow it intentionally, and protect it legally, you do not just accumulate; you activate.

* * *

BOTTOM LINE:

Money is not the destination. It is the vehicle.

And the more efficiently you drive it, especially through intelligent tax strategy, the farther you can go.

QUESTIONS TO REFLECT AND RECALIBRATE

1. **What is your earliest memory about money?** (*How did that experience shape your current financial mindset?*)
2. **When you think about money, what emotion rises first: excitement, fear, indifference, or control?** (*Awareness is the first step toward change.*)
3. **How did your family, mentors, or culture talk about money when you were young?** (*Did they see it as security, struggle, or success?*)
4. **Do you view money as something to chase, control, or collaborate with?** (*That answer determines whether you live reactively or proactively.*)
5. **If money were a person, what kind of relationship would you have?** (*A supportive partner, an unpredictable friend, a distant stranger?*)
6. **What would your life look like if you could keep 20-30+ percent more of what you earn, legally and strategically?** (*How would that impact your practice, your family, and your community?*)

7. **Where could your extra tax savings create the greatest ripple effect?** *(Investing in your business, your people, your purpose?)*

8. **Where in your life are you respecting money, and where might you be neglecting or idolizing it?** *(Balance begins with awareness.)*

9. **What new story do you want to write about your relationship with money starting today?** *(Every financial transformation begins with a mental one.)*

PART V
ECONOMICS, REALITY &
PRESCRIPTION

UNDERSTANDING THE SYSTEM IS THE
FIRST STEP TO MASTERING IT

Here, you'll connect the dots between policy, markets, and mindset—
and walk away with your prescription for peace of mind and purpose.

CHAPTER 17

❧

THE CURRENT ECONOMICS OF MEDICINE & TAX POLICY

"In the middle of difficulty lies opportunity." —*Albert Einstein*

"Tax laws change. Your principles shouldn't. Build flexibility into your strategy, and you'll thrive regardless of who's in the White House." —*Paavan Kotini*

THE CURRENT ECONOMICS OF
MEDICINE & TAX POLICY

⚜

*D*r. Sarah Chen was having coffee with her financial advisor when her phone buzzed. Subject line: "**URGENT: Major Tax Changes Coming in 2025.**"

She glanced at it, sighed, and put her phone back on the table. "Let me guess," she said. "Another tax law shift I'm supposed to panic about?"

Her advisor smiled. "Or, you do what you've always done —build strategies that work regardless of what happens in Washington."

This chapter is not about predicting politics. It's about preparing **financial defenses** in an age where medicine is changing, tax codes are shifting, and **artificial intelligence** is accelerating how the IRS reviews, audits, and enforces compliance.

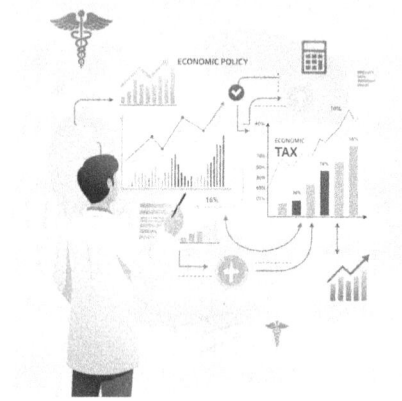

Figure 17.1: Understanding economic trends and tax policy helps doctors anticipate shifts and build resilient strategies.

* * *

WHAT WE KNOW (As of Late 2025)

The **2017 Tax Cuts and Jobs Act (TCJA)** reshaped the tax landscape for individuals and businesses. It lowered the top marginal rate to 37%, nearly doubled the standard deduction, and introduced a 20% deduction for qualified business income (QBI). Those benefits were scheduled to expire after 2025—just as new legislation, the **One Big Beautiful Bill Act (OBBBA)**, was signed into law on **July 4, 2025,** permanently rewriting much of the tax narrative.

1. What Was Originally Set to Expire

Before the OBBBA, several TCJA provisions were set to **sunset** and revert to pre-2017 law:

- **Top marginal rate:** 37% → 39.6%
- **Standard deduction:** nearly doubled → reduced to prior lower levels
- **Child tax credit:** reduced
- **Mortgage-interest deduction:** tighter limits reinstated

- **SALT deduction:** remained capped at $10,000
- **QBI deduction:** 20% pass-through deduction → eliminated
- **Estate & gift exemption:** ~$13.6 million → ~$7 million per person
- **Bonus depreciation:** 100% → 60% (2024) → 40% (2025) → 20% (2026) → 0% (2027)

For many high-income physicians and practice owners, this could have meant tens of thousands in additional annual taxes.

2. The One Big Beautiful Bill Act Changed Everything

The **OBBBA**, enacted July 4, 2025, effectively prevented the "sunset storm" and locked in several key provisions—while introducing new incentives designed to boost investment, innovation, and middle-class stability.

Provision	Old TCJA Sunset (Pre-2026)	OBBBA Update (July 2025)	Impact on Doctors & Dentists
Top Individual Rate	Would have reverted to 39.6%	**37% made permanent**	Predictable planning for high-income professionals
Standard Deduction	Would have been cut roughly in half	**Made permanent**	Simpler filing and sustained tax savings
SALT Cap	Remained $10,000	**Raised to $40,000 (2025-2029)**, then $10,000	Short-term relief for high-tax-state professionals
QBI Deduction (§199A)	Set to expire 12/31/2025	**Made permanent and increased to 23% (starting 2026)**	Greater benefit for S-Corp and LLC practice owners
Bonus Depreciation	Scheduled phase-out to 0% by 2027	**Permanently restored to 100% for qualified property placed in service on or after Jan 20, 2025**	Major boost for equipment, technology, and real estate reinvestment
Estate & Gift Tax Exemption	Would have dropped ~50% in 2026	**Made permanent and raised to $15 million per person (indexed)**	Expanded wealth-transfer planning window
New Deductions	N/A	**Added deductions for tips and overtime**	Meaningful for dental and medical practices with variable staffing

Figure 17.2: The key provisions of the One Big Beautiful Bill Act and impact on doctors and dentists.

3. What Could Have Happened—and Why You Still Plan for Multiple Scenarios

In early 2024, Dr. Lisa Chen's CPA modeled three possible outcomes:

Scenario 1 — Full TCJA Expiration (Did Not Happen)

Rates rise, QBI ends, estate exemption shrinks → ≈ $40k + higher annual tax exposure.

Scenario 2 — OBBBA Extension (What Happened)

Rates stay at 37%, QBI rises to 23%, SALT cap $40k, bonus depreciation returns to 100%, estate exemption expands.

Scenario 3 — Partial Extension (Hybrid)

Some provisions renewed, others scaled back.

Lisa didn't try to predict policy—she prepared for all three. That flexibility paid off when OBBBA passed.

Your Action Plan: Building Tax-Agnostic Strategies

1. Maximize Benefits Under Current Law

Take advantage of what's available now:

- Max out qualified-plan and retirement contributions.
- Accelerate practice investments while 100% bonus depreciation applies.
- Complete cost-segregation studies for owned real estate.
- Execute 1031 exchanges where appropriate.

2. Build Flexibility Into Your Financial Structure

Bucket	Examples	Tax Now	Tax Later
Tax-Deferred	Traditional 401(k), Cash Balance Plan, SEP IRA	$0	Ordinary rates
Tax-Free	Roth IRA, Roth 401(k), HSA, IGLI	Regular rates	$0
Taxable	Brokerage account, real estate, practice ownership	Varies	Capital gains rates

Figure 17.3: *Think in **three tax buckets**. Tax-Deferred, Tax-Free, and Taxable.*

"You can't control future tax rates," Lisa's advisor told her. "But you can control *when* and *how* your dollars are taxed."

3. Model Multiple Scenarios With Your CPA

Revisit projections quarterly. The OBBBA shifted assumptions overnight—those who modeled ahead adjusted in days, not months.

4. Stay Informed Without Overreacting

Dr. James Park spent hours trying to forecast Washington. He missed deductions, mistimed purchases, and stressed himself out. Lisa stayed focused on fundamentals and adjusted only when laws actually changed.

"Tax laws evolve, but the fundamentals don't," Lisa said. "Maximize deductions, minimize taxable income, and stay proactive."

AI and the New IRS Reality

The IRS is no longer a paper-driven bureaucracy—it's a data-driven operation powered by AI. Machine-learning systems now analyze:

- Unusual or inconsistent deductions
- Underreported income patterns
- Lifestyle vs. practice income discrepancies
- Benchmark deviations among high-income professionals

Physicians and dentists—once under the radar—are now among the most closely monitored taxpayer groups.

- Electronic medical-practice systems mirror reported income.
- Practice sales automatically trigger capital-gain alerts.
- AI compares industry averages to individual filings in real time.

The new rule: If your strategy isn't documented, sourced, and provable, AI will flag it before a human ever sees it.

* * *

BOTTOM LINE: The *Sunset Storm* has passed, but the era of **Smart Compliance and Strategic Coordination** has arrived.

Build a plan that's flexible, defendable, and proactive—and you'll sleep well at night no matter who writes the next bill.

* * *

*2025 AND BEYOND: **The Sunset Storm—Recalibrated***

*When the **Tax Cuts and Jobs Act (TCJA)** passed in 2017, it set the stage for one of the most sweeping tax overhauls in decades—but with a built-in expiration date. Many of its most valuable provisions were scheduled to "sunset" at the end of 2025, threatening to roll back key tax advantages for physicians, dentists, and small business owners.*

For years, financial planners called it the Sunset Storm: the point where lower rates, expanded deductions, and higher exemptions could all vanish overnight unless Congress intervened.

That storm never fully arrived.

*In **July 2025**, the **One Big Beautiful Bill Act (OBBBA)** changed the landscape yet again—making many of the TCJA's most impactful provisions **permanent** and even expanding a few.*

* * *

How the Rules *Have Shifted*

Provision	Original TCJA Sunset (Pre-2026)	Updated Under OBBBA (July 2025)	Impact on Doctors & Dentists
Individual Income Tax Rates	*Scheduled to revert to higher pre-2017 brackets*	*Made **permanent** under OBBBA*	*Predictable long-term planning for high-income professionals*
20% QBI Deduction (Section 199A)	*Set to expire after 2025*	*Made **permanent***	*Pass-through practices keep full deduction benefits*
Estate & Gift Tax Exemption	*Scheduled to drop by roughly 50% in 2026*	*Made **permanent and increased** to **$15 million per person** (indexed for inflation)*	*Expanded legacy and wealth-transfer opportunities*
Bonus Depreciation	*Phased down from 100% → 60% (2024) → 40% (2025) → 20% (2026) → 0% (2027)*	***Permanently reinstated at 100%** for qualified property placed in service on or after **Jan 20, 2025***	*Major boost for practice expansion, equipment purchases, and real estate investments*

Figure 17.4: Breakdown of how the rules have shifted from the original TCJA to the OBBA and the impact it has on doctors and dentists.

* * *

What This Means Going Forward

While the feared Sunset Storm has largely passed, the lesson remains the same: **proactive planning pays dividends.**

For doctors and dentists, these legislative changes cement an era of opportunity—stable tax brackets, expanded deductions, and reinforced incentives to reinvest in your practice, your family, and your future.

But permanence in law doesn't mean permanence in life.

Markets shift. Administrations change. Tax policy evolves.

The key is to stay coordinated, stay informed, and keep your **Doctors Family Office (DFO)** *engaged to ensure each piece of your plan continues to glide in sync—calm, deliberate, and designed to help you* **Sleep Well At Night.**

The goal is not to predict. The goal is to prepare.

* * *

PRINCIPLES OVER POLICY

Doctors who panic over policy changes lose power. Doctors who **plan for all outcomes** gain control.

Your strategy must be portable —able to survive red, blue, or gridlock.

* * *

WILL THE **IRS** BE ABOLISHED?

The idea of eliminating income taxes and replacing the IRS with an "External Revenue Service" might sound enticing at first-who wouldn't love a world without tax day? Recently, President Donald Trump floated the concept of funding the federal government entirely through tariffs instead of income taxes. But let's look at why that proposal is highly unlikely to become reality, at least for now.

To replace the roughly **$3 trillion** the U.S. collects annually from income taxes, tariffs on imported goods would need to skyrocket-estimates range from **100% to 200%** on *all imports*. That would cause consumer prices to surge, reduce demand, and incentivize domestic production. And here's the catch: if imports decline, so does tariff revenue. The very mechanism intended to replace taxes would collapse under its own weight.

Beyond economics, the IRS is deeply woven into the legal and financial infrastructure of the federal government. It's not just a tax collector-it administers credits, enforces compliance, manages federal funding flows, and underpins countless financial regulations. Removing it isn't a policy tweak; it's a constitutional overhaul.

In short, while the headline may sound bold, proposals to abolish the IRS often serve as a political message, conveying that tax collection will continue in some form no matter what the agency is called.

* * *

Questions to Think About

1. **Am I building my tax plan around permanent principles or temporary provisions?** *(Temporary provisions can vanish. Permanent principles persist.)*
2. **What happens to my tax bill if major provisions expire?** *(Have your CPA model both best-case and worst-case scenarios.)*
3. **Am I letting political uncertainty prevent action?** *(Uncertainty is permanent in tax policy. Action creates certainty.)*
4. **Do I have a tax strategy that survives IRS AI review?** *(Is your strategy documented, sourced, and provable —does it have a tax opinion, private letter ruling, or is it codified?)*
5. **Am I acting like tax law is permanent —or preparing like it's temporary?** *(Don't assume anything is permant, esp in the tax code—in addition to the IRC, the overall tax code framework also includes: Treasury regulations, IRS publications and guidance, & Court cases. All of which are constantly changing)*

* * *

Questions to Ask Your CPA

1. **What happens to my tax bill under different legislative scenarios?** *(Your CPA should model multiple outcomes so you understand the range of possibilities.)*

2. **Which strategies should we implement now, regardless of legislative changes?** *(Focus on strategies with lasting value.)*

3. **How can we build flexibility into my plan to adapt to different policy scenarios?** *(This includes balancing W-2 and pass-through income, maintaining multiple tax buckets, and creating reversible strategies where possible.)*

* * *

THE BOTTOM LINE

Tax laws will continue to change. The OBBB illustrates how quickly rules can shift. Predicting election outcomes or legislative details is not a viable strategy.

Instead, focus on actionable fundamentals:

- Maximize deductions and credits available now
- Build a flexible financial structure
- Model multiple scenarios
- Stay informed without succumbing to fear

By emphasizing principles over politics, doctors can thrive under any administration.

Bottom Line: Political winds change. Proactive planning does not. Proactive planning beats perfect prediction every time.

* * *

ADDITIONAL INSIGHTS & ACTION STEPS

The current economic environment shapes the future of your wealth more than any single tax strategy. As of late 2025, the U.S. national debt has surpassed **$38 trillion** and continues to rise. Interest rates remain elevated to control inflation, while federal spending pressures mount from healthcare, energy transition, and defense commitments.

The conversation around taxation has shifted from *if* rates will rise to *when* and *how much.*

For physicians, dentists, and high-income professionals, ignoring these macroeconomic realities is like ignoring a patient's vital signs—it's not optional, it's diagnostic.

* * *

THE POLICY BACKDROP: **TCJA and OBBBA**

The **2017 Tax Cuts and Jobs Act (TCJA)** originally lowered individual tax rates and doubled the standard deduction, but many of its provisions were set to expire after 2025.

The **One Big Beautiful Bill Act (OBBBA)**, passed in mid-2025, **made several of those benefits permanent**—including the 37% top bracket, the 20% QBI deduction, and 100% bonus depreciation.

But permanence in legislation doesn't mean permanence in policy direction. Rising deficits have already sparked debate about **surtaxes on high earners**, **new wealth taxes**, and **adjustments to capital gains treatment**. Flexibility—not prediction—will be your greatest asset in the coming decade.

* * *

RETIREMENT PLANS AND **SECURE 2.0: The New Rules of the Game**

The **SECURE 2.0 Act**, fully implemented in 2025, reshaped the retirement landscape—especially for physicians and business owners.

Key provisions to note:

- **Mandatory Roth Catch-Up Contributions:**
- If your **W-2 wages exceeded $145,000** in the prior year, your **catch-up contributions must now be made as Roth**, not pre-tax.
- Ages **50–59:** $7,500 Roth catch-up.
- Ages **60–63:** $11,250 Roth catch-up (the new "super catch-up" tier).

- This change impacts most high-earning physicians and dentists, effectively shifting part of your retirement savings into **tax-free growth territory**.
- **Increased RMD Age:**
- The age for **Required Minimum Distributions (RMDs)** rises to **75** by 2033, giving you more runway for Roth conversions and tax-efficient withdrawals.
- **Employer Matching Flexibility:**
- Employers (including your own practice) can now make **Roth contributions for matches**, creating new hybrid plan opportunities for owner-operators.
- **Automatic Enrollment and Escalation:**
- New 401(k) and 403(b) plans must auto-enroll employees at **3–10%** of pay, increasing annually up to **15%**—a quiet but powerful nudge toward higher savings rates.

* * *

PROACTIVE PLANNING **in a Shifting Landscape**

1. Stay Informed (but not reactive)

Subscribe to financial and policy resources that interpret—not sensationalize—legislation. Reliable outlets include the **Tax Foundation, Kitces.com**, and the **AICPA Tax Section**.

2. Build Tax-Agnostic Strategies

Prioritize flexibility. Combine **Roth accounts, permanent life insurance, municipal bonds,** and **real estate depreciation** to create a portfolio that performs under multiple tax regimes.

3. Model Multiple Scenarios

Work with your CPA or Virtual Family Office (VFO) team to project your cash flow under different tax environments. If marginal rates rise 5%, or capital gains shift to ordinary treatment, how would that alter your after-tax retirement income? Scenario modeling turns uncertainty into clarity.

4. Diversify Beyond Borders

U.S. fiscal tightening may contrast with growth abroad. Consider allocating a portion of your portfolio to **global equities, infrastructure, and real assets** to hedge against domestic tax and currency risk.

5. Preserve Liquidity and Optionality

Keep part of your portfolio **liquid and accessible.**

Liquidity equals leverage—the ability to pivot quickly when opportunities or risks appear. Illiquidity, by contrast, can lock you into a suboptimal plan just when flexibility matters most.

* * *

THE BOTTOM LINE

Understanding policy isn't about predicting the future—it's about positioning yourself to thrive across *multiple* futures.

Medicine evolves. Tax law evolves. Wealth strategies must evolve with them.

Your greatest advantage won't come from knowing every new rule —it will come from **having a coordinated plan and a proactive team** ready to adapt when the rules change.

CHAPTER 18

S.W.A.N. APPROACH TO STOP FINANCIAL
BLEEDING

"A good financial plan is a road map that shows us exactly how the choices we make today will affect our future."— Alexa Von Tobel

"Financial bleeding doesn't stop with more income—it stops with more intention. The S.W.A.N. Approach isn't about making more money; it's about making your money make more sense."— Paavan Kotini

S.W.A.N. APPROACH TO STOP FINANCIAL BLEEDING

*E*verything in this book comes down to one guiding principle: helping you **Sleep Well At Night (S.W.A.N.)** Not just financially—but holistically.

Because true wealth isn't only about higher returns or bigger numbers on a balance sheet. It's about peace of mind, clarity of direction, and confidence in the plan that protects what you've built.

I've been using the S.W.A.N. philosophy for over twenty years when crafting strategies for families. And though it has evolved, its essence has never changed: to create financial lives built on clarity, control, and calm.

When most people think about investing, they picture two animals —the bull and the bear. One charges forward with optimism, the other retreats with caution. But both, to me, always felt aggressive— symbols of reaction, not reflection.

So I envisioned something different. Something graceful. Purposeful. Steady.

That's where **S.W.A.N.** was born—a mindset centered on designing your financial life like a swan gliding across the water. Calm on the surface. Disciplined and deliberate beneath.

It's not about chasing every opportunity or fearing every downturn. It's about planning for the best, preparing for the worst, and remaining composed through both. That balance—between boldness and prudence—is what allows you to truly sleep well at night.

S = Security

Your family is protected. Your assets are shielded. Your income streams are diversified. Security isn't fear-based—it's freedom-based. You sleep better when your downside is covered.

W = Wealth

Not just high income, but real wealth—assets that grow, compound, and transfer to the next generation. True wealth is what continues to serve your family long after you stop working.

A = Alignment

Your financial strategies align with your values, your goals, and your stage of life. When your money and mission move in sync, every decision feels lighter and more intentional.

N = No Regrets

You're not waking up at 2 a.m. wondering if you missed something or overpaid someone. No regrets doesn't mean perfect—it means confident. You've done the work, and it shows.

S.W.A.N. isn't just a financial framework—it's a philosophy. It's about creating a life where your money serves your mission, not your anxiety. When you lead with clarity, align with purpose, and protect what matters, you don't just build wealth—you build peace.

That's the ultimate return on investment: to live boldly, plan wisely, and truly sleep well at night.

Figure 18.1: When your financial life is in order, you can sleep well at night knowing your wealth is protected.

* * *

THE S.W.A.N. Test

Can you answer "yes" to these questions?

- If I couldn't practice medicine tomorrow, would my family be financially secure?
- Am I confident I'm not overpaying taxes by six figures?
- Do I have a coordinated team—or am I still the coordinator?
- Am I building wealth that will outlast me?
- Can I focus on medicine without constant financial stress?

If you answered "yes" to all five, congratulations—you've built a strong foundation. Now imagine how much stronger it could be with a true **Doctors Family Office** guiding, coordinating, and elevating every part of your plan.

If you answered "no" or even "maybe" to any, that's not failure—it's feedback. You now know where to focus, and you don't have to do it alone. The roadmap—and the right partners—are within reach.

* * *

The Bottom Line

You became a doctor to heal people—not to become a financial coordinator, not to stay up late reading tax code, and not to wonder if your CPA and financial advisor are even on the same page.

Build or hire your team. Implement the strategies.

Sleep Well At Night.

That's what you've earned. That's what you deserve.

* * *

Additional Insights & Action Steps

S.W.A.N.—Sleep Well At Night—captures the essence of true wealth.

It's not defined by the size of your bank account but by the calm you feel knowing your family is cared for, your risks are managed, and your values are reflected in every financial decision.

In a profession where sleepless nights are common, designing your finances to promote restful sleep might be the most compassionate thing you can do for yourself.

S.W.A.N. has two dimensions: **practical and psychological.**

Practically, it means having your asset allocation, insurance coverage, and estate plan dialed in so unexpected events don't derail your life.

Psychologically, it means releasing the anxiety that comes from the unknown—by educating yourself, aligning your spending with your values, and setting boundaries around how much time you devote to money matters.

Take Dr. Lee, an oncologist who realized her sleeplessness had less to do with market volatility and more to do with guilt—about not spending enough time with family. After reviewing her finances, she cut unnecessary expenses, increased contributions to her kids' education funds, and planned a sabbatical funded by a side business. The result wasn't just stronger numbers—it was peace of mind.

To cultivate your own **S.W.A.N.:**

- **Define what "enough" means.** How much do you truly need to feel secure? Clarity reduces anxiety.

- **Set guardrails.** Choose an allocation you can live with through market ups and downs. Diversify across asset classes and time horizons.

- **Protect your human capital.** Ensure adequate disability and life insurance so your earning power and legacy remain intact.

- **Automate generosity.** Giving regularly to causes you care about reminds you that money is a tool, not a scorecard.

- **Schedule financial check-ins.** Once a quarter, review your plan. Outside of that, give yourself permission not to worry.

S.W.A.N. isn't an overnight achievement. It's the compound result of hundreds of small, intentional choices—each one creating a little more clarity, confidence, and calm.

Start today. Tomorrow's sleep will feel that much sweeter.

CHAPTER 19

❧

BRINGING IT ALL TOGETHER

"True wealth isn't built in silos. It's orchestrated: when every move, every advisor, every dollar plays in harmony toward one vision." —Paavan Kotini

"The whole is greater than the sum of its parts." —Aristotle

BRINGING IT ALL TOGETHER

*here is a moment in every physician's life when the pieces finally connect. When what once felt like random symptoms form a clear diagnosis. This book has been building toward that same moment of clarity, because your financial health deserves the same precision you bring to your patients.

Over the past eighteen chapters, we have walked through the anatomy of your financial life. From how the system quietly drains high-income earners, to the proven strategies that help you stop the bleed. We diagnosed the problem, explored the causes, and prescribed a plan for recovery. Now it is time to step back, take a deep breath, and see the whole body of work together.

* * *

THE DIAGNOSIS

It began with awareness. You learned that income is not the same as wealth, just as a heartbeat is not the same as health. The big lie is that earning more will fix financial stress. But the truth is that without proactive planning, higher income often leads to higher taxes and higher pressure.

Through the stories of Dr. Michael and Dr. Arjun, you saw how two equally talented professionals could end up worlds apart financially. One filed. The other planned. One hoped things would work out. The other made them work out.

Awareness was the first treatment. Action became the cure.

* * *

THE TREATMENT PLAN

You discovered that every effective tax plan rests on three pillars: deductions, credits, and depreciation. Once you understood these, the tax code stopped looking like a maze and started to look like a map. You saw how small, consistent wins, when applied year after year, compound into millions in wealth.

You learned that structure matters. Entities, trusts, and retirement accounts are not just paperwork. They are protection. They are the surgical instruments of wealth creation. For doctors and dentists, the 7702 plan, the micro-captive, and the defined benefit plan are not exotic tricks. They are tools that can build a foundation for tax-free or tax-efficient income for decades.

You also saw that timing matters. Whether buying equipment, selling a practice, or investing in real estate, proactive timing can turn a tax bill into a wealth strategy.

* * *

THE MINDSET SHIFT

You saw that health and wealth share one simple truth: prevention beats reaction. The same discipline that helps you diagnose early, manage risk, and design treatment applies to your financial life. The goal is not to hoard wealth. It is to design freedom. To have the time and mental space to focus on what truly matters: your family, your mission, and your peace of mind.

You began redefining your relationship with money. Seeing it not as the root of stress or status, but as energy. A resource to steward wisely. You realized that mitigating taxes is not greed. It is steward-ship. It is your civic responsibility to manage your resources effi-ciently so you can do more good with what you keep.

* * *

THE BIG PICTURE

Each chapter has been a lens. Together, they form the full picture: a proactive framework where your tax strategy, investments, insur-ance, entity structure, and purpose all align.

This is the essence of the S.W.A.N.™ Approach, Sleep Well At Night. It is not just about saving taxes. It is about building clarity, confidence, and continuity. It is about turning chaos into calm, complexity into simplicity, and money into meaning.

You now have the tools, the mindset, and the structure to take control of your financial future. But knowledge alone does not change your life. Implementation does.

* * *

THE TRANSITION Forward

The next chapter is where information becomes transformation. It is where you turn strategy into action, and theory into results. Whether you are just starting, rebuilding, or preparing to scale, your next step determines your outcome.

Because no patient ever healed from reading a treatment plan. They healed when they followed it.

So take a breath. Reflect on what you have learned. Then let's bring it all together, and take it one step further.

CHAPTER 20

THE NEXT STEP

"The future depends on what you do today."—Mahatma Gandhi

"You've read the book. You understand the strategies. Now it's time to act." —
Paavan Kotini

THE NEXT STEP

*T*here is a saying in medicine: "The prescription means nothing if the patient never takes it."

You have made it this far through the diagnosis, the data, and the design. You now know that wealth is not built by chance but by choice. You have seen how doctors who plan differently live differently. This is the point where insight becomes action.

Knowledge without execution is like a brilliant treatment left on the table. The next chapter of your financial life is not about learning more. It is about doing differently.

Figure 20.1: Your journey doesn't end here; continue taking informed steps toward a brighter financial future.

* * *

STEP ONE: Get a True Financial Diagnosis

Before any surgeon operates, they study the chart. They gather data and confirm the full picture before making a single incision. Your financial life deserves the same care.

Start with a complete diagnostic review: income streams, entity structures, tax returns, insurance policies, investments, and estate documents. Do not assume these pieces are working together. Most professionals have a patchwork of advisors who rarely speak to each other. That is where the bleeding begins.

Ask yourself:

- Do I know my true effective tax rate for the past three years?

- Are my CPA, attorney, and financial advisor coordinating their efforts?
- Do I have a single plan that connects tax, risk, and wealth?

If any of these answers make you hesitate, that hesitation is your starting point.

* * *

STEP TWO: Build or Hire Your Dream Team

Every successful procedure depends on collaboration. Surgeons, anesthesiologists, nurses, and specialists work in sync toward a single outcome. Financial health deserves the same precision.

Yet most physicians unknowingly operate with fragmented advisors. The CPA looks backward. The financial advisor watches markets. The insurance agent manages policies. The attorney drafts documents. Each does good work—but few see the entire patient.

That's why we created the **Doctor's Family Office (DFO)** model.

At Kotini & Kotini, the DFO brings coordination where confusion once ruled. We don't view taxes, investments, and insurance as separate silos. We see them as an integrated system—one that, when aligned, builds clarity, confidence, and ultimately freedom.

Your DFO acts as the financial quarterback, orchestrating every play and ensuring all parts of your financial life move in concert. Just as a primary physician coordinates care across specialists, we coordinate your financial strategy across every advisor.

The goal is simple: stop the financial bleeding, preserve more of what you earn, and build the legacy you envisioned when you first put on your white coat.

You can assemble your own team—it takes time, trial, and often error. Or you can partner with a coordinated team that already plays in rhythm. In the end, your most valuable asset isn't money—it's time. The right team gives you more of it.

I invite you to a free discovery session with me, with no strings attached. Let's explore your financial dreams, discuss your objectives, and craft a personalized plan that aligns with your unique aspirations. Reach out to me at paavan@kotiniandkotini.com or call 804-372-8307 to begin the conversation.

Step Three: Move from Reactive to Proactive

Most doctors live in a constant state of reaction. The tax bill arrives, the market dips, or a new investment appears, and decisions are made in haste. Proactivity is the antidote.

Proactive planning means working on the future before it arrives. It means making tax decisions in the spring that pay off next winter. It means creating business structures that serve you, not just the IRS.

Ask questions like:

- How can I reduce next year's taxes by taking action this quarter?

- What income can be shifted into more efficient entities?

- How can I pre-fund future liabilities through structures like 831(b) captives, 7702 plans, or charitable LLCs?

This is how you replace uncertainty with peace of mind.

* * *

Step Four: Align Purpose and Prosperity

Money is a powerful servant but a poor master. True wealth is about alignment. It is about connecting your financial plan with your personal mission.

For one doctor, that might mean creating a scholarship fund or supporting global health initiatives. For another, it may mean building a family trust or buying back time to be present with loved ones.

The goal is not to chase the biggest number. The goal is to build the most meaningful life.

That is the core of the S.W.A.N.™ philosophy: Sleep Well At Night.

When your tax plan, risk strategy, and purpose are working together, you trade financial anxiety for calm confidence.

* * *

THE TWO PATHS

You are standing at a fork in the road.

Path 1: Close this book, go back to your life, and keep doing what you have always done. Keep being a Filer instead of a Planner. Keep watching 35 to 45 percent of your income disappear to taxes every year. Retire with a good life, but always wonder what could have been.

Path 2: Take action. Implement these strategies. Build your team. Become a Planner. Save six or seven figures in taxes over your career. Retire with the wealth you have earned, not just what is left after Uncle Sam takes his share.

Which path will you choose?

* * *

ONE FINAL STORY

Last year, I met with a 62-year-old orthopedic surgeon. Let's call him Dr. Stevens. He was two years from retirement, and he was stressed.

"Paavan," he said, "I have been a doctor for 35 years. I have earned over fifteen million dollars in my career. But I only have two and a half million saved. Where did it all go?"

I pulled up his tax returns. Over 35 years, he had paid nearly five million in taxes. Another seven and a half million had gone to living expenses, his kids' education, and lifestyle.

He had earned fifteen million. He had kept two and a half.

"What if you had implemented just three strategies from this book?" I asked. "What if you had done cost segregation on your rental properties, set up a Cash Balance Plan, and created a side consulting LLC?"

I ran the numbers. Conservatively, he would have saved two million in taxes over his career.

His two and a half million would have been four and a half. An eighty percent increase.

He looked at me and said quietly, "I wish I had met you twenty years ago."

I do not want you to say that twenty years from now.

* * *

THE MISSION HASN'T CHANGED

I got into medicine because I wanted to help people.

I could not stop the physical bleeding, but I found a way to stop the financial bleeding.

My family eventually gave me the name 'Financial Doctor' or 'Tax Doctor' (different from my sister who went on to become an ER medical doctor.)

The strategies are here. The roadmap is clear. The only question left is whether you will take action.

You have spent years earning your income. Now it is time to keep it.

Stop the bleeding.

Build your wealth.

Live the life you have earned.

Let's get to work.

* * *

THE BOTTOM LINE

You would never perform surgery with half your instruments.

You shouldn't build wealth with half a plan.

You now have the insight, the structure, and the mindset. The next step is partnership.

Build your **Doctors Family Office.**

Build your **peace of mind.**

Build your **legacy.**

* * *

ADDITIONAL INSIGHTS & Action Steps

Reaching the final chapter isn't the end of your journey—it's the launchpad for everything that comes next. The choices you make in the coming weeks will determine whether the knowledge you've gained becomes transformative or merely interesting.

Information without action is like an unused prescription—it can't heal.

Treat your financial life like a patient under your care. Diagnose its condition. Prescribe targeted interventions. Monitor progress and refine as you go. Don't aim for perfection; aim for continuous, compounding progress.

Here's your blueprint for taking action:

- **Schedule an initial strategy session.** Meet with your advisory team within the next month. (If you don't have one —hire a DFO. You deserve it.) Bring your notes from this book and articulate your top priorities.

- **Create a plan.** Identify two or three high-impact actions— forming an entity, opening a new retirement account, or exploring a real estate strategy—and put deadlines on your calendar.

- **Educate yourself further.** Choose one focus area—trusts, depreciation, or alternative investments—and commit to reading or attending a workshop. (See Appendix F for recommended resources.)

- **Share your goals.** Tell a trusted colleague or partner what you plan to accomplish. Accountability amplifies follow- through.

- **Revisit and refine.** At year's end, review what worked and what didn't. Adjust and set fresh targets for the next quarter.

The most successful doctors I know aren't the ones who consume endless financial content—they're the ones who decide, act, and iterate.

Your next step doesn't have to be dramatic. It just has to be yours.

Take it today—and experience the compounding power of forward motion.

EPILOGUE: THE DOCTOR WHO STOPPED THE BLEEDING

*L*et me take you back to where we started.

I couldn't become the oncologist I set out to be. I couldn't handle the sight of blood.

But I discovered a different kind of bleeding-financial bleeding-and I found a way to stop it.

Over the past two decades, I've had the privilege of working with hundreds of physicians just like you. Brilliant, hardworking, compassionate people who spent years training to heal others-but who were getting destroyed by taxes.

I've seen doctors earning $500,000 a year who felt broke.

I've seen specialists working 80-hour weeks who couldn't get ahead.

I've seen practice owners generating millions in revenue who watched half of it disappear to Uncle Sam.

And I've seen what happens when those same doctors learn the strategies in this book:

- The hospitalist who saved $60,000 in taxes in Year 1 by implementing a side business structure and cost segregation study

- The surgeon who deferred $2 million in capital gains taxes using a 1031 exchange
- The dermatologist who saved $300,000 in estate taxes by setting up an ILIT
- The practice owner who contributed $200,000/year to a Cash Balance Plan, saving $80,000 annually in taxes

These aren't theoretical stories. These are real doctors who took action.

And now it's your turn.

* * *

The Difference Is Intentionality

The difference between Dr. Michael Anderson and Dr. Arjun Mehta-the two doctors whose stories bookended this journey-wasn't intelligence. It wasn't luck. It was intentionality.

You're standing at the same crossroads they faced.

You can be Michael-earning well, saving what you can, hoping for the best.

Or you can be Arjun-planning proactively, implementing strategies, building a coordinated team.

The choice is yours.

* * *

My Promise to You

I promised at the beginning of this book that I wouldn't waste your time.

I promised every strategy would be practical, legal, and implementable.

I promised clear action steps.

I promised you'd see yourself in these stories.

Have I delivered?

If so, I have one final request: **Act.**

Don't let this book sit on your shelf. Don't let these strategies remain theoretical. Don't let another year go by where you overpay taxes by six figures.

You've earned your income. Now keep it.

* * *

The Invitation

If you're ready to stop the bleeding, if you're ready to build your wealth, if you're ready to Sleep Well At Night, we're here to help.

At Kotini & Kotini, we've spent two decades building the infrastructure, the team, and the systems to help doctors just like you implement everything in this book as your DFO.

We're not for everyone. We work best with doctors who:

- Earn $400,000+ and pay over $100,000+ in taxes
- Are tired of being reactive and ready to be proactive
- Value coordination over isolated advice
- Want a team, not just vendors

If that's you, let's talk.

Visit our website, schedule a free consultation, and let's see if we're a fit.

Because you became a doctor to heal patients-not to coordinate financial advisors.

* * *

The Final Word

I couldn't become the oncologist I dreamed of being.

But I found my purpose anyway-helping doctors like you stop the financial bleeding so you can focus on what you do best: healing people.

The mission hasn't changed. Only the method has.

Now go build the wealth you've earned.

Sleep Well At Night.
And never overpay taxes again.
Paavan Kotini
Founder, Kotini & Kotini
Creator of the original Doctor's/Dentists Family Office
paavan@kotiniandkotini.com or call 804-372-8307

*Aim your Phone's camera to the QR code above to have access to the
links for my webpage, social media, email and other links.*

APPENDIX A: THE DENTIST'S/DOCTOR'S CHECKLIST FOR TAX-EFFICIENT WEALTH & RISK MITIGATION

*Use this checklist to evaluate your current financial strategy, identify opportunities, and ensure both **wealth growth and protection.***

Level 1: Basic Deductions & Foundation

☐ Max out 401(k)/403(b) ($23,000 or $30,500 with catch-up)

☐ Max out HSA ($8,300 family or $4,150 individual)

☐ Backdoor Roth IRA contributions ($7,000 per person)

☐ Track all deductible expenses (subscriptions, CE, licenses, uniforms, etc.)

☐ Maintain an emergency fund (6–12 months of expenses)

☐ Review and optimize debt structure (refi, interest deductibility, etc.)

Level 2: Side Business Structure & Efficiency

☐ Form LLC for side income (consulting, speaking, moonlighting, etc.)

☐ Elect S-Corp status (if net income > $50,000)

☐ Deduct home office expenses appropriately

☐ Deduct business travel and professional development

☐ Operate Solo 401(k) or SEP with profit sharing

☐ Evaluate accountable plan reimbursements for tax-free benefits

Level 3: Tax Credits & Charitable Planning

☐ Utilize Energy Asset Tax Mitigation Strategy (28–40% federal)

☐ Use historic preservation credits (20% federal + state)

☐ Contribute to a Donor-Advised Fund (DAF)

☐ Donate appreciated assets (stock, crypto, real estate—not cash)

☐ Explore Qualified Charitable Distributions (QCDs) if over 70½

Level 4: Depreciation & Accelerated Deductions

☐ Own rental real estate and track all expenses

☐ Complete cost segregation studies for bonus depreciation

☐ Leverage Section 179 for equipment and vehicles

☐ Qualify spouse as Real Estate Professional (REPS) when applicable

Level 5: Advanced Retirement & Tax-Free Buckets

☐ Explore Cash Balance or Defined Benefit Plans

☐ Evaluate Mega Backdoor Roth contributions

☐ Use insurance-based retirement (7702 plans) for tax-free accumulation

☐ Coordinate employer plans with private wealth strategies

Level 6: Risk Mitigation & Protection

☐ Maintain adequate term and/or permanent life insurance (income replacement, liquidity, legacy)

☐ Evaluate disability insurance (own-occupation coverage, true residual rider)

☐ Review long-term care (LTC) or hybrid life-LTC solutions

☐ Maintain umbrella liability coverage (consider $2–5M+)

☐ Use key-person or buy-sell insurance for business partners

☐ Establish Irrevocable Life Insurance Trust (ILIT) for estate liquidity

☐ Consider 831(b) micro-captive plan for business owners to self-insure risk (malpractice, cyber, equipment, etc.)

☐ Regularly stress-test all policies for adequacy and alignment with tax and estate strategy

Level 7: Real Estate & Asset Strategies

☐ Execute 1031 exchanges to defer capital gains

☐ Qualify short-term rentals via material participation

☐ Track REPS hours and documentation for compliance

☐ Integrate Opportunity Zone or Delaware Statutory Trust (DST) investments where appropriate

Level 8: Estate, Legacy & Continuity

☐ Maintain updated will and trust (revocable and/or irrevocable)

☐ Title assets correctly (avoid probate, ensure liquidity)

☐ Explore advanced trusts: Charitable Remainder, GRAT, SLAT, and Dynasty structures

☐ Coordinate ILIT and 831(b) ownership structures for multi-entity families

☐ Review beneficiary designations annually

Level 9: Team Coordination & Governance

☐ Engage proactive CPA who plans year-round

☐ Work with a financial strategist who integrates tax, legal, and insurance

☐ Have an estate attorney who coordinates across disciplines

☐ Conduct annual strategy session with full team

☐ Hold quarterly check-ins for proactive adjustments

☐ Document all key relationships, passwords, and continuity plans

Annual Rhythm for the Proactive Professional

Quarter 1:

- *Review prior year tax return for missed deductions*
- *Increase retirement plan contributions to match IRS limits*
- *Review credit reports and optimize debt*

Quarter 2:

- *Meet with team to refine estimated taxes*
- *Reassess insurance and risk coverage (life, disability, LTC, umbrella, 831(b))*
- *Fund your charitable strategy or DAF*

Quarter 3:

- *Review investments and rebalance portfolio*
- *Evaluate real estate (cost seg, 1031, leverage)*
- *Assess 831(b) claim utilization or premium planning*

Quarter 4:

- *Finalize year-end retirement, charitable, and tax strategies*
- *Execute tax-loss harvesting*
- *Update estate documents and insurance beneficiaries*

Ongoing Action Steps

☐ Automate savings and policy premiums

☐ Digitize and store key documents securely (trusts, wills, policies, buy-sell agreements)

☐ Engage your spouse or partner in financial decisions

☐ Celebrate progress and milestones. Financial wellness is cumulative

* * *

Bottom Line:

A checklist isn't bureaucracy —it's brilliance. It's how surgeons prevent mistakes and prevent disasters. For doctors and dentists, it's how wealth turns from accidental to intentional. Protect first, plan proactively, and position your wealth to **grow, guard, and give.**

APPENDIX B: READING YOUR 1040 LIKE A RADIOLOGIST

When a radiologist studies an image, they don't just glance at the surface—they trace patterns, identify shadows, and look for what isn't there. Your Form 1040 deserves the same diagnostic eye. It's more than a tax return; it's a financial X-ray revealing what's healthy, what's stressed, and what opportunities are being overlooked.

* * *

Step 1: The Intake Scan — Lines 1 to 8 (Income Sources)
This is the "patient history" of your financial life.

- Line 1: W-2 income—how much of your effort is still taxed at the highest rates.

- Line 2–3: Interest and dividends—shows whether your money is working efficiently or just parking in taxable accounts.

- Line 4: IRA, pensions, annuities—are distributions being managed or forced?

- Line 7: Capital gains—did you harvest intelligently, or reactively?

- Line 8: Other income—rental, pass-through, or side ventures worth deeper imaging (often the richest source of deductions).

Doctor's Note: High W-2 income with little Schedule C or E activity often signals untapped planning potential.

* * *

Step 2: The Contrast Dye — Adjustments and Above-the-Line Deductions (Lines 10–15)

These lines show what the IRS lets you subtract before arriving at Adjusted Gross Income (AGI).

Think of them as the "contrast dye" that clarifies flow.

- Contributions to HSAs, retirement plans, SEP-IRAs, or self-employed health insurance tell you where pre-tax opportunities are being used—or missed.

- Student loan interest or educator expenses often fade early in a physician's career but reveal where phaseouts start.

* * *

Step 3: The Core Image — Adjusted Gross Income (Line 11)

Your AGI is the vital sign that drives nearly every tax calculation. It determines eligibility for Roth IRAs, child credits, 199A deductions, and Medicare surcharges. If your AGI is chronically high, it's like an elevated blood pressure reading—you may feel fine, but long-term strain is building.

* * *

Step 4: The Differential Diagnosis — Deductions and Credits (Lines 12–20)

- Itemized vs. Standard: Are you capturing all deductible interest, taxes, and charitable contributions—or defaulting to standard because documentation feels painful?

- Qualified Business Income (QBI): For practice owners, this is your 20% deduction lifeline—if structured correctly.

- Credits: Child, education, and energy credits are the "preventive medicine" of tax planning.

* * *

Step 5: The Prognosis — Tax, Payments, and Refund (Lines 22–37)
Here's where the story resolves.

- Tax liability shows your true exposure.
- Payments and withholding reflect whether your plan was proactive or reactive.
- A large refund isn't a win—it's proof of an interest-free loan you gave the government.

Doctor's Note: Aim for precision dosing: owe slightly or break even each April, not a penny more.

* * *

Step 6: The Follow-Up — Schedules and Attachments
The supporting schedules are like MRI slices—they reveal depth:

- Schedule C: Your business or side practice—look for

missing deductions (home office, mileage, continuing education).

- Schedule E: Rentals and pass-throughs—often where depreciation and cost segregation can change outcomes.
- Schedule A: Itemization patterns that hint at overlooked charitable or medical strategies.

* * *

Step 7: The Treatment Plan — From Data to Diagnosis

Reading a 1040 isn't about compliance; it's about pattern recognition. When you see recurring "pain points"—high W-2, minimal deductions, rising AGI—it's time for intervention:

- Shift income character from active to passive.
- Introduce advanced retirement or insurance strategies (Cash Balance, 7702, 831(b)).
- Align your CPA, advisor, and attorney into one integrated team—your financial care consortium.
- Refer to the IRS website for the latest updates on the 1040 form (https://www.irs.gov/forms-pubs/about-form-1040).

* * *

Key Takeaway

A radiologist doesn't just report what's visible—they interpret what it means. Likewise, a proactive planner doesn't just file a 1040—they diagnose, prescribe, and monitor. When you learn to read your return like a radiologist, you stop reacting to taxes and start treating your wealth like your most important patient.

APPENDIX C: QUESTIONS TO ASK WHEN INTERVIEWING A CPA

Not all CPAs are created equal. Use these questions to find a proactive tax planner (not just a tax filer).

1. **"How many physicians do you work with?"** (You want someone who specializes in high-income professionals.)
2. **"What's your approach to tax planning vs. tax preparation?"** (You want someone who plans proactively, not just file returns.)
3. **"How often will we meet throughout the year?"** (You want at least quarterly meetings, not just once a year.)
4. **"Can you give me an example of a proactive tax strategy you've implemented for a client similar to me?"** (This shows whether they think strategically.)
5. **"Do you have a family office offering or coordinating with financial advisors and estate attorneys?"** (You need a team player, not a silo.)
6. **"What's your experience with cost segregation studies, Cash Balance Plans, and 1031 exchanges?"** (These are advanced strategies every high-income doctor should know about.)

7. **"What's your fee structure?"** (Proactive planning costs more than basic filing-but it should have a clear ROI.)
8. **"Can you show me a sample tax projection?"** (Good CPAs create projections so you're never surprised in April.)
9. **"How many CPA's are on your team and do you all have capacity for more complex tax planning?"** (If they have very little team and high volume, that just churns tax filing then they won't have time for the more advanced planning).

APPENDIX D: GLOSSARY OF PROACTIVE TAX & WEALTH TERMS

1031 Exchange: A strategy that allows you to sell investment property and defer capital gains taxes by reinvesting proceeds into a like-kind property.

1040: The primary IRS form for individual income tax returns — essentially your annual "financial X-ray," summarizing income, deductions, credits, and taxes owed or refunded.

179 (Section 179): Tax code provision that allows you to deduct the full cost of qualifying equipment or vehicles in Year 1 (up to $2.5 million post-OBBB).

7702: A section of the Internal Revenue Code defining how life insurance policies qualify for tax advantages. It determines whether policy cash value grows tax-deferred and can be accessed tax-free through loans.

831(b): A section of the tax code that allows small businesses to create "micro-captive" insurance companies — a legitimate risk management vehicle that can also generate tax advantages when structured properly.

Backdoor Roth: A strategy that lets high-income earners contribute to a Roth IRA by making a non-deductible traditional IRA contribution and converting it to Roth, bypassing income limits.

Bonus Depreciation: Allows you to deduct a large percentage (currently 100% post-OBBB) of the cost of qualifying assets in Year 1.

C-Corporation: A business structure discussed alongside S-Corporations that allows profits to be taxed separately from owners and can offer fringe benefits and lower corporate rates when properly structured.

Capital Gain: The profit from selling an asset (like real estate, stock, or a business) for more than its purchase price. Taxed at either short-term or long-term capital gains rates.

Cash Balance Plan: A type of defined-benefit retirement plan that allows contributions far exceeding 401(k) limits.

Charitable Remainder Trust (CRT): A trust that allows you to donate assets, receive a partial tax deduction, and retain income from those assets for life or a set term — with the remainder going to charity.

Cost Segregation: An engineering study that accelerates depreciation by reclassifying building components into shorter depreciation schedules.

Credit: A dollar-for-dollar reduction of your tax liability (stronger than a deduction). A $1,000 tax credit reduces your tax bill by $1,000.

Deduction: An expense subtracted from income before taxes are calculated — reducing your taxable income, not your actual tax bill.

Depreciation: The gradual deduction of an asset's cost over its useful life — representing wear, tear, and obsolescence. In planning, it's a non-cash expense that creates real tax savings.

DFO (Doctor/Dentist Family Office): A specialized Virtual Family Office designed for dentists, physicians, or other healthcare professionals, integrating tax, legal, insurance, and wealth strategies under one coordinated umbrella.

Donor-Advised Fund (DAF): A charitable account that allows you to make a contribution, receive an immediate tax deduction, and recommend grants to charities over time.

Effective Tax Rate: Your total tax divided by your total income — the real-world percentage of income you pay in taxes.

Estate Planning / Estate Tax Exemption: The coordinated process of arranging assets, entities, and trusts to transfer wealth efficiently and minimize estate taxes within IRS exemption limits.

HSA (Health Savings Account): A triple-tax-advantaged account for medical expenses — tax-deductible contributions, tax-free growth, and tax-free withdrawals.

Income Tax: The tax you pay on earned and unearned income, based on federal and (in most states) local tax brackets.

Irrevocable Life Insurance Trust (ILIT): A trust that owns life insurance, keeping the death benefit out of your taxable estate.

Leveraged Charitable Donation: A strategy using financing (often through a donor-advised or charitable series LLC) to amplify charitable impact and deductions — effectively "giving with leverage."

Marginal Tax Rate: The tax rate you pay on your last dollar of income — your highest bracket.

OBBB (One Big Beautiful Bill): A reference to the comprehensive tax legislation following the 2017 Tax Cuts and Jobs Act. Often called the "Tax Cuts 2.0," it consolidated multiple budget extensions and technical corrections into one sweeping update. The OBBB reinforced and expanded provisions such as bonus depreciation, Section 179 limits, and certain small-business deductions while phasing in adjustments to corporate and individual tax rules. For proactive planners, it represents the bridge between the original TCJA and the next evolution of U.S. tax reform.

Opportunity Zone (QOZ): A designated area where investors can defer, reduce, or even eliminate capital gains taxes by investing in qualified development projects.

Ordinary Income: Income taxed at regular marginal rates — includes wages, interest, and business earnings.

QBI (Qualified Business Income Deduction): A deduction (up to 20%) for eligible business owners on pass-through income — designed to level the field with corporate rates.

Real Estate Professional Status (REPS): IRS classification allowing rental real estate losses to offset active income — powerful for high-income investors.

Reasonable Salary: The IRS-required standard that an S-Corporation owner must pay themselves fair compensation before taking distributions to avoid reclassification of income.

Revocable Living Trust: A flexible estate-planning tool that allows assets to bypass probate while retaining control during the grantor's lifetime.

Roth IRA: A retirement account offering after-tax contributions with tax-free growth and withdrawals if qualifying conditions are met.

SALT (State and Local Taxes): Deduction for state income, property, and sales taxes — currently capped at $10,000 per year federally.

S-Corporation: A tax election that allows business income to be split between salary (subject to payroll tax) and distributions (not subject to self-employment tax).

S.W.A.N. (Sleep Well At Night): Paavan's trademarked guiding philosophy — building wealth strategies that create confidence, clarity, and calm through proactive planning.

Tax Cuts and Jobs Act (TCJA): The landmark 2017 legislation that redefined tax brackets, deductions, and business provisions — many of which are set to sunset in 2026.

Traditional IRA: A retirement account allowing pre-tax contributions with tax-deferred growth until withdrawal.

VFO (Virtual Family Office): An integrated, tech-enabled wealth model combining tax, wealth, risk, legal, business advisory, insurance, and investment services into one coordinated advisory experience.

APPENDIX E: BIBLIOGRAPHY

Primary Government & Regulatory Sources

- *Internal Revenue Service (IRS). (2025). Internal Revenue Code Sections 401(k), 408A, 7702, 831(b), 1031, 199A, and related Treasury Regulations. U.S. Department of the Treasury.*

- *Internal Revenue Service (IRS). (2025). Guidance on the One Big Beautiful Bill Act (OBBBA).*

- *U.S. Bureau of Labor Statistics (BLS). (2025). Occupational Employment and Wage Statistics.*

- *U.S. Department of Energy. (2025). Residential Clean Energy Credit and Efficiency Incentive Guidelines.*

- *U.S. Department of Commerce, Census Bureau. (2025). Professional Services and Small-Business Economic Outlook Report.*

- *Social Security Administration. (2025). Contribution and Benefit Base Limits.*

- *U.S. Department of the Treasury. (2025). Qualified Opportunity Zone ("QOZ 2.0") Final Regulations.*

Professional & Medical Associations

- *American Medical Association (AMA). (2025). Physician Compensation Report 2025.*

- *Medscape. (2025). Physician Compensation and Lifestyle Report 2025. WebMD LLC.*

- *American Dental Association (ADA) Health Policy Institute. (2025). Survey of Dental Practice and Economic Outlook 2025–2026.*

- *American Veterinary Medical Association (AVMA). (2025). Economic State of the Veterinary Profession 2025.*

- *Pro-Fi 20/20 Dental CPAs. (2025). Tax Insights for Dental and Medical Practices.*

Economic & Financial Research

- *Tax Foundation. (2025). Post-OBBBA Tax Policy Briefs and Historical U.S. Federal Income Tax Rates.*

- *Tax Policy Center (Urban-Brookings). (2025). Distribution of Federal Taxes and Effective Rates.*

- *Forbes Finance Council. (2025). Strategies for High-Income Taxpayers Under the One Big Beautiful Bill Act.*

- *Harvard Business Review. (2024). The Psychology of Financial Decision-Making and Wealth Behavior.*

Legislation & Acts

- *One Big Beautiful Bill Act of 2025 (Pub. L. No. 118-203).*

- *Tax Cuts and Jobs Act of 2017 (Pub. L. No. 115-97).*

- *Tax Reform Act of 1986 (Pub. L. No. 99-514).*

- *Revenue Act of 1964 (Pub. L. No. 88-272).*

Academic & Published Authors Cited

- *Franklin, B. (1789). Letter to Jean-Baptiste Le Roy (on death and taxes).*

- *Holmes Jr., O. W. (1880). The Simplicity Beyond Complexity Essay.*

- *Kiyosaki, R. T. (1997). Rich Dad Poor Dad. Warner Books.*

- *de Saint-Exupéry, A. (1943). The Little Prince. Reynal & Hitchcock.*

- *Eisenhower, D. D. (1957). Speech to National Defense Executives on Planning and Preparation.*

- *Calvin, K. (2012). Giving and Impact: Philanthropy as Social Change. UN Foundation.*

Industry & Practice-Specific References

- *831(b) Institute. (2025). Micro-Captive Insurance and Risk Management in the Post-OBBBA Era.*

- *IRS Notice 2025-02 and Rev. Proc. 2025-11. Micro-Captive and Alternative Risk Structure Compliance Guidance.*

- *National Association of Insurance Commissioners (NAIC). (2025). Indexed Universal Life Market Report.*

- *Opportunity Zone ("QOZ 2.0") Guidelines. (2025). U.S. Department of the Treasury Final Regs TD 9991.*

Secondary Citations & Illustrative Sources

- *Gapin, T. (2021). Male 2.0 and Codes of Longevity. High-Performance Press.*

- *Kotini, P. (2023). Effortless Wealth: The S.W.A.N. Approach to Unlocking Wealth for Busy Professionals. Kotini Press.*

- *Interise. (2023). StreetWise MBA Program Curriculum Guide.*

- *The Wharton School. (2023). Entrepreneurship Acceleration Program Overview.*

APPENDIX F: RECOMMENDED RESOURCES

FOR CONTINUING EDUCATION, DEEPER LEARNING & INSPIRED ACTION

* * *

Books on Wealth, Mindset, and Tax Strategy

Effortless Wealth – *Paavan Kotini*
A practical guide to achieving financial clarity and peace of mind through the S.W.A.N.™ (Sleep Well At Night) philosophy—integrating tax efficiency, risk management, and purposeful planning.

The Psychology of Money – *Morgan Housel*
An insightful exploration of why people make the financial decisions they do—and how behavior often outweighs intelligence in building lasting wealth.

The Art of Proactivity – *Anton Anderson & Paul Lathem (Foreword by Paavan Kotini)*
A modern look at proactive financial advisory models and the shift toward integration, collaboration, and holistic client outcomes.

The White Coat Investor – *Dr. James Dahle*

A cornerstone resource for physicians and healthcare professionals navigating the unique financial and tax challenges of medical practice.

Tax-Free Wealth – *Tom Wheelwright, CPA*

A straightforward explanation of how the tax code rewards entrepreneurs and investors who plan strategically and align their actions with government-favored incentives.

Tax-Free Retirement – *Patrick Kelly*

An accessible introduction to using life insurance and other tax-advantaged tools to create income streams that can be withdrawn tax-free in retirement.

The Power of Zero – *David McKnight*

A clear roadmap to positioning assets for a potentially zero-tax retirement, leveraging Roth accounts and permanent life insurance strategies.

The Simple Path to Wealth – *J.L. Collins*

A timeless guide to financial independence through disciplined investing, minimalism, and intentional lifestyle design.

Rich Dad Poor Dad – *Robert T. Kiyosaki*

A mindset classic contrasting active income and asset-based wealth, emphasizing how understanding the tax code can accelerate independence.

* * *

Websites & Continuing Education Platforms

KotiniandKotini.com

The home of the Doctors Family Office (DFO). Access educational resources, tax strategy insights, and proactive planning tools designed for physicians, dentists, and business owners.

IRS.gov

Official IRS source for publications, forms, and current guidance on Sections 179, 199A, 1031, 831(b), 7702, and related provisions.

WhiteCoatInvestor.com

Community and blog created by Dr. James Dahle offering physician-focused financial education, investing insights, and practice-owner advice.

Kitces.com

Michael Kitces' in-depth resource for financial planners and tax professionals seeking advanced content on strategy design and legislative updates.

TaxFoundation.org

Independent analysis of tax policy changes, historical rates, and the economic impact of major legislation such as the TCJA and OBBBA.

Investopedia.com

Straightforward explanations of complex financial and tax concepts—ideal for reference or quick clarification.

* * *

Professional & Industry Organizations

American Institute of CPAs (AICPA.org)

Leading professional association for CPAs with continuing education, tax guidance, and practice management resources.

National Association of Tax Professionals (NATPTAX.com)

Focused on practitioner-level education and compliance updates for tax preparers, advisors, and CPAs.

Financial Planning Association (OneFPA.org)

A professional network of planners committed to advancing fiduciary, client-centered financial planning practices.

American Dental Association (ADA.org) & American Medical Association (AMA-ASSN.org)

Essential policy and economic resources for clinicians integrating business ownership and practice management into their careers.

* * *

Podcasts, Media & Ongoing Learning

Effortless Wealth? Prove It. – *Hosted by Paavan Kotini*

Candid conversations with thought leaders, physicians, and entrepreneurs on proactive wealth design, purpose-driven business, and the mindset of modern financial freedom.

Financial Symmetry Podcast – *Hosted by Chad Smith & Allison Berger*

Explores behavioral finance and practical strategies for sustainable wealth building.

Money Guy Show – *Brian Preston & Bo Hanson*

Real-world discussions connecting tax strategy, investing, and life planning in a relatable way.

The Merriman Financial Education Podcast – *Paul Merriman*

Evidence-based insights on portfolio design, diversification, and retirement distribution strategies.

Aim your Phone's camera to the QR code above to have access to the links for my webpage, social media, email and other links.

APPENDIX G: BEFORE YOUR FIRST FAMILY OFFICE CONSULTATION

Congratulations.

You have taken the first step toward proactive planning and the peace of mind that comes from true financial clarity.

Just as every great diagnosis starts with good data, your Family Office journey begins with preparation. The more complete your picture, the more precise your strategy.

Use this readiness checklist to organize the key documents, details, and intentions that will help your DFO team design a plan tailored to you.

1. Core Financial Documents
Gather the most recent versions of the following:

- Last two to three years of personal and business tax returns (Form 1040 and business filings)

- W-2s, 1099s, and K-1s for all income sources

- Practice financial statements (profit and loss, balance sheet, and cash flow)

- Personal balance sheet listing assets, liabilities, and ownership percentages

- Recent brokerage and retirement account statements (401(k), IRA, SEP, Defined Benefit Plan)

- Life insurance and disability policies (with cash values and premium details)

- Trust or estate planning documents, including wills or living trusts

- Real estate documents (deeds, rental schedules, loan statements, and cost segregation studies if any)

2. Business and Entity Structure

Provide details for any entity you own or manage:

- Entity type (LLC, S-Corp, C-Corp, Partnership, PLLC, etc.)

- Ownership percentages and partners (if applicable)

- EIN and state of formation

- Operating agreements or bylaws

- Any existing 831(b), captive, or defined benefit plan structures

3. Income and Expense Snapshot

To help identify deductions and opportunities:

- Average annual income (physician salary, distributions, consulting income)

- Estimated annual tax liability and effective tax rate

- Major deductions currently used or missed

- Personal and practice expenses that may qualify for tax optimization

4. Goals and Priorities

Spend a few quiet minutes on this section. It guides everything that follows.

- What does financial freedom look like for you?

- Are you planning to expand, sell, or transition your practice?

- What keeps you up at night financially?

- What legacy do you want your work to fund, family, philanthropy, or both?

- How do you define "Sleep Well At Night" in your own words?

5. Team and Advisor Roster

List every current professional you work with:

- CPA or tax preparer

- Financial advisor or wealth manager

- Attorney (estate, business, or contract)

- Insurance agent or risk advisor

- Banker or lender

Include contact information so your Family Office can coordinate efforts and eliminate duplication or conflict.

6. Mindset and Commitment

Ask yourself:

- Am I ready to shift from reactive to proactive?

- Am I open to a team approach where specialists collaborate for my benefit?

- Am I willing to measure results and stay accountable to the plan?

If your answer is yes, you are ready for your Family Office consultation.

* * *

Final Thought

You have spent years building your practice. Now it is time to build your peace of mind.

Bring these materials to your first consultation, and together we will design a strategy that protects what you have built and multiplies what is possible.

You can hire a family office—or build your own. But not all are created equal.

If this book resonated with you, explore Kotini & Kotini, the original creators of the Doctors Family Office— Where doctors and dentists plan boldly, live fully, and preserve wisely.

Cheers,

Paavan Kotini

Aim your Phone's camera to the QR code above to have access to the links for my webpage, social media, email and other links.

ACKNOWLEDGMENTS

This book exists because of the hundreds of physicians who've trusted me with their financial lives over the past two decades. Thank you for allowing me to be part of your journey, to help you heal more than patients, but the financial stress that too often follows purpose-driven work.

To my powerhouse team at Kotini & Kotini, with a special shoutout to **Aleigha Chandler** and **DaQuan Morris** you both turn "what if" into "what's done." Your integrity fuels the mission, and your excellence turns vision into reality. Proud is an understatement.

To my incredible partner, **Madhuri**, thank you for standing beside me through every pivot and possibility, for believing in futures not yet visible, and for caring for me as lovingly as a third child (sometimes more than I deserve).

To my amazing children, **NityaNidhi and Premsai**, you both are my daily reminder of why potential should never be postponed. You make life joyful, unpredictable, and full of wonder.

To my mentor, **Anton Anderson**, whose generosity of time, wisdom, and unwavering belief in proactive planning has profoundly shaped both my practice and my purpose. Your lessons continue to echo through everything I build.

To my first publisher, **Paul McManus**, for turning *Effortless Wealth* from an idea into authorship. You opened the door that allowed my words to find their wings and gave me the confidence to let them fly.

To my life mentor, **Sri Sathya Sai Baba**, who has guided me through moments of doubt and darkness, and illuminated my path with his eternal philosophy: *Love All, Serve All. Help Ever. Hurt Never.*

You remind me daily that the true measure of success is living with purpose, compassion, intent and the courage to reach one's fullest potential.

And to every doctor reading this: thank you for the lives you save, the sacrifices you make, and the service you give. You've earned the right to keep more of what you build. **Now go make it happen.**

ABOUT THE AUTHOR

Paavan Kotini is the visionary strategist and founder of **Kotini & Kotini**, a boutique **Virtual Family Office (VFO)** dedicated to helping first-generation wealth builders, high-net-worth families, and entrepreneurs **Sleep Well At Night (S.W.A.N.™)** through proactive, multi-disciplinary planning.

With nearly two decades in the financial services industry, Paavan has earned a reputation for transforming complex financial challenges into clear, actionable pathways. His career began far from finance-in **biomedical engineering at Vanderbilt University**, where he cultivated the analytical precision and scientific discipline that now underpin his approach to wealth, tax, legal, and risk strategy.

After seven years in **cancer research**, a pivotal moment-an unexpected encounter in the lab-changed his path forever. Realizing that he couldn't stomach blood but could stop another kind of bleeding, **he pivoted to finance to help people stop financial hemorrhaging**.

Since entering the industry in 2007, Paavan has guided hundreds of doctors and professionals to save millions in taxes, grow sustainable wealth, and design lives of financial freedom. His work culminated in the creation of "**The Doctor's/ Dentist's Family Office**"-a coordinated, team-based approach to financial care inspired by the collaborative model of medicine itself.

Paavan is an **Accredited Virtual Family Office Professional**, holds a **StreetWise MBA® from Interise** and completed the **Entrepreneurship Acceleration Program at The Wharton School**, sharpening his expertise in business strategy, leadership, and innovation. This rare combination of engineering rigor, entrepreneurial insight, and virtual family office accreditation fuels his ability to craft plans that are both structurally sound and forward-looking.

A **best-selling author of** *Effortless Wealth*, Paavan is also the host of the **podcast** *Effortless Wealth? Prove It.*, where he explores real stories of wealth, wisdom, and purpose. He recently wrote the foreword to *The Art of Proactivity*, underscoring his mission to spark new conversations about designing wealth with intention.

At his core, Paavan is a connector-bridging disciplines, people, and ideas to create clarity where others see complexity. He lives with his family and remains devoted to the mission that started it all: **helping people live better, plan smarter, and sleep well at night.**

AFTERWORD

A SMALL REQUEST

If *Tax-Efficient White Coat: The S.W.A.N.™ Approach How Doctors & Dentists Can Stop the Tax Bleed and Build Real Wealth* has given you a fresh perspective on taming taxes and building real wealth, I'd be incredibly grateful if you'd take a moment to share your thoughts with an Amazon review. Your feedback not only supports my work but also helps other physicians and dentists find the path to financial clarity-and maybe even a few more restful nights.

Know a colleague or family member trapped in the quicksand of complex finances? Perhaps a busy doctor or dentist looking to treat their tax troubles and set their finances on a healthier course? Consider sharing *Tax-Efficient White Coat* with them. You can even gift it directly on Amazon—because sometimes the best prescription is knowledge.

THE END

www.ingramcontent.com/pod-product-compliance
Lightning Source LLC
Chambersburg PA
CBHW070348200326
41518CB00012B/2173